More Praise for *Forgive and Be Free*

"The class we had in San Quentin with Ana opened up many doors, leading us to freedom and a deeper sense of self—even behind bars. This book contains valuable teachings on peace for everyone, no matter where you've been or what you've done."

—Kevin Penn, former San Quentin inmate for 23 years, now offering peace education and substance abuse prevention in California.

Forgive
and Be
Free

About the Author

Ana Holub, MA (Mount Shasta, CA), is a forgiveness counselor, author, poet, and peace educator. She holds a BA in Peace Studies and an MA in Dispute Resolution from Pepperdine University School of Law. Ana is also a certified domestic violence counselor and Radical Forgiveness coach. She's deeply inspired by her daily study of *A Course in Miracles*, meditation, and yoga. From her own difficult childhood to becoming a successful counselor, Ana knows firsthand the benefits of using forgiveness as a tool for inner peace and freedom. Over the past twenty years, she's worked with thousands of people, including women, men, teens, couples, government, at-risk families, prison inmates, nonprofits, businesses, and schools.

Ana teaches workshops internationally on forgiveness, emotional healing for couples, recovery from addiction, and women's issues. Her work includes *The Edges Are Friendly* (poetry), *The Healing Power of Forgiveness* audio CD, and three e-courses: *Letting Go with Forgiveness, Claiming Your Emotional Well-Being,* and *Blessings from A Course in Miracles.*

Ana teaches her clients practical skills for living boldly in harmony, strength, and empowerment. Visit her online at AnaHolub.com.

Ana Holub

Forgive
and Be
Free

A Step-by-Step Guide
to Release, Healing,
and Higher Consciousness

Llewellyn Publications
Woodbury, Minnesota

First Edition
First Printing, 2014

Book design by Donna Burch
Cover art: iStockphoto.com/14138702/STILLFX/10722337/pagadesign
Cover design by Kevin R. Brown
Editing by Andrea Neff

Llewellyn Publications is a registered trademark of Llewellyn Worldwide, Ltd.

Library of Congress Cataloging-in-Publication Data
Holub, Ana, 1961–
  Forgive and be free : a step-by-step guide to release, healing, and
higher consciousness / by Ana Holub. — First edition
      pages cm
  Includes bibliographical references.
  ISBN 978-0-7387-3617-4
  1. Forgiveness—Religious aspects. I. Title.
  BL65.F67H65 2014
  202'.2—dc23
                                                                    2013038923

Llewellyn Publications
A Division of Llewellyn Worldwide Ltd.
2143 Wooddale Drive
Woodbury, MN 55125-2989
www.llewellyn.com

Printed in the United States of America

Dedication

For my parents, Suzanne and Donald Holub.

*May you continue to fly with the angels
and experience the peace of God forever.*

Acknowledgments

I thank Master Jesus, who gave us *A Course in Miracles*, and the ancient and modern teachers who expand the wisdom of divine love. Special appreciation goes to the Radical Forgiveness community, and to Colin Tipping for introducing me to forgiveness as a healing path and to the idea of making forgiveness lists.

The teaching and ideas of Michael Joslin, Pitaka Christie Close, Iris Lambert, Peter Van Dyk, and Peter Levine have immeasurably deepened my understanding of healing modalities in breathwork, accessing intuition, counseling, and peace education. Thanks to Peter Van Dyk for his help in formulating H.O.W. with me. I am grateful for the groundbreaking scientific and social ideas of Bruce Lipton, Candace Pert, Byron Katie, and Michael Gurian. To my writing team: Michael Carr, Linda Sivertsen, Natalie Kottke, Jen Mathews, and my agent, Jeff Herman—thank you! Where would I be without you?

To the team at Llewellyn Worldwide, especially Angela Wix—thanks for taking a chance on me. And finally, I thank the circle of people who love and support me, whether they understand me or not: my incredible children, Amalia Holub and Aron Lucas; my sisters, Melissa and Kathy Holub; my friends Marguerite Ogle, Donna Bringenberg, Thea Kristina Kenegos, Jen

Mathews, Prajna Ami Marcus, Gentle Thunder, Sarah Alexander, Jack Moore, Mona Therese Winston, Amy Cooper, Andrew Oser, and Richard Lucas; and my extended community in Mount Shasta and beyond. I love you all.

Contents

Preface

It was summer. I was on a river trip with a group of women, all of us adventuring together on the Klamath River in far northern California, up near the Oregon border. I was paddling my kayak, drinking in the day, the beauty, the dappled sunshine glinting on the water's surface. Underneath, though, I was worried. What if I got tossed?

Every serious river runner has to deal with this fear at some point. I'd been paddling the Klamath for years, a dozen times or more, managing to stay in the boat through countless rapids and getting pretty handy in the process. I'd "gone swimming" only once before, years back. But I knew that at some point the river would swoosh my little body out of the boat again and leave me floundering in the rush-and-tumble current, because that's just how it is. You can't do a lot of river running without that experience, and the more I kayaked, the closer I came to the inevitable.

I was lucky—it was a warm day. Coming up to a midsized rapid, I paddled hard to align my boat with the perfect slot to slide from smooth water into the churning torrent. As so often happens in whitewater, the slightest drop in my concentration would be my undoing. I darted a glance to "river right," making sure to avoid some overhanging branches, then put my focus back on the slot ahead of me.

But that one glance cost me a microsecond I didn't have, and the river wasn't waiting around. I went sideways over the rapid, rolled upside down, and got shucked out of that little kayak so fast I couldn't even think about it. I was swimming, and that was that. The water was zipping me along, my bright yellow boat bobbing merrily off to my left.

After the first shock of surprise, magic happened. I realized that the mighty Klamath River was holding me, carrying me, buoying me up. I felt utterly safe in its embrace, and out of the blue, I began to cry. My warm, salty tears met the sparkling river water, and we celebrated the truth that in this moment, there was nothing wrong, nothing scary, nothing to shrink from or avoid—just warm water carrying me downstream. The river felt strong and steadfast, covering all of me but my upturned face and knobby knees. As it took me, I relaxed into the safety of it, still crying with relief and new understanding. It was a moment I will never forget.

Kayaking or rafting can be a dangerous sport, and not every toss from a boat in swift water leads to an experience as ecstatic as mine on that wondrous summer day. Just the same, I learned a powerful lesson from the Klamath. All my fears, hesitations, and assumptions were laid bare in one drenching, cathartic moment, when I realized they were not true. The lesson was powerful because I was so aware of the metaphor: the water embracing me was alive and teaching me to trust, just as every moment is alive, embracing me and welcoming me to let go, forgive my fears, and trust in life itself. That day, I found out that the river of life is also the river of love.

Exploring Forgiveness

Perhaps you're interested in the potential of forgiveness in your life, but you wonder, "If I forgive, does that mean I'm weak? Does it mean I'll turn into a sap, or a clone, or a doormat? Will people use and abuse me if I forgive? Do I need to forget what happened, or will I become too passive or 'airy fairy' if I forgive?" The answer is NO to all of that. Forgiveness is actually a workout for the soul to make you stronger *and* more loving and compassionate at the same time. As Mahatma Gandhi once said, "The weak can never forgive. Forgiveness is an attribute of the strong."

The forgiveness method you'll find in this book teaches us how to embrace our emotions—all of them—

and lead ourselves back to conscious union with our Creator. We bond with Spirit and we don't let go. We apply ourselves to the discipline of uncovering what is false and releasing our attachment to falsehood. We commit ourselves utterly to awakening—our number one priority.

In some ways, especially in the Western world, understanding emotion and including it in our spiritual path is a novel idea. In the past forty years, some of us have jumped into hatha yoga and sitting meditation with delight, swimming blissfully in our newfound Eastern wisdom. But after the yoga class or the meditation retreat, we've gone home to deal with shaky finances, unruly time management, the mysteries of sex, child rearing, temper tantrums, addictions, broken relationships, painful memories, the habitual griping and complaining that seem to be the norm in our society— and in no time, the ecstatic state we were in has evaporated and becomes ever more elusive. Any of this sound familiar? This is why forgiveness is so crucial to our healing. We simply can't leave it out.

How Forgiveness Moves in Me: A Personal Introduction

I first became attracted to the healing arts, especially meditation and yoga, during my college years. I had already spent a lot of time as a dancer, so I was familiar with moving, stretching, and strengthening my body.

Yoga was different, though, and I found it a perfect complement to my new passion for meditation.

With hatha yoga (the yoga of movement using poses called *asanas*), I needed to slow down and to tune in to my breath, my fears, and my prayers. I found a teacher named Christine and began eagerly attending her classes. Early on, she said something that really surprised me. I remember it well. She said, "Things may come up for you in yoga class. Emotional things. Don't talk to me about it." That was it!

I was confused. If "things" were going to come up for me, and Christine wasn't interested in helping me, who would? I admired Christine's honesty, and I was happy to know that she wasn't the person to turn to, but she didn't offer another choice. And being young and naive, I didn't ask for one—I just kept showing up for yoga class.

Perhaps one of the reasons I remember Christine's comment so clearly is that on that day, a seed was planted inside me. It took some time to grow, but twenty-five years later, I would be called to write a book about forgiveness and emotional healing. I feel this book fills a need, because emotional release is a subject that many people are just beginning to explore. Even if you've done a lot of therapy, yoga, or meditation, there will probably be some inner stretch for you in your forgiveness process. In this classroom, we're all equal students of life.

There are plenty of people who don't attend yoga or meditation classes and who are nonetheless experiencing lots of spiritual openings in their lives. If we're experiencing a spiritual awakening, then we are students of Spirit, whether or not we ever attend a single class. The opening of our true inner nature is popping up everywhere these days, in every country, in every sphere and stratum of society. *This book is written for everyone who wants to consciously forgive, connecting their emotional experiences with their deep opening to the divine.*

For the past twenty-odd years, I've taught peace education in schools, prisons, and businesses as well as in seminars and private sessions. In peace education, I include not only forgiveness work, but also communication skills, gender healing, anger management, and breathing techniques for stress reduction. I guide people of all ages, shapes, sizes, cultures, political persuasions, and educational backgrounds, and I have seen the path we all tread. Again and again, I've seen similarities in people behind bars and in business suits, kids in a regular classroom and in juvenile hall, and couples in love and at the brink of divorce. What matters is our willingness and sincerity to seek the truth. Like magic, sincerity clears the way for precious gems of wisdom to rise up from the depths of our inner knowing.

We're all on a surprisingly archetypal path. The ways we walk it have common symbolism and direction, and a scope much larger than any one person's journey. It is from this gathered research and insight into the emotional and spiritual realms that I offer this book. It's for you.

What Is Forgiveness?

In committing to our path of freedom, we need to examine what forgiveness is, and what it's not. In the traditional view of forgiveness, a common element is that some grave offense has been committed. If there was no crime, there's no need to forgive! So if you feel that forgiveness is what's next for you, you'll need to find the "crimes" in your life story. *By "crime," I mean any action (or perhaps a lack of action) taken by yourself or someone else that seemed to cause you pain, sadness, fear, or some other emotion that you didn't want to feel at the time.* It could be something as violent as a rape or murder, or as small as a nasty look or icy silence.

I say "seemed to cause you pain" because it's never the physical actions that make us feel bad, but rather how we *interpret* the situation. It's possible for one person to feel terrible anguish over something that someone else would scarcely even notice. Even dramatic acts of violence can have different effects on different people, depending upon what those involved *think* about what happened. Our emotions stem from and join with our thinking. Always.

We have a choice in how we interpret our surroundings and how we interpret the intentions of others. We can choose fear or love. If we choose fear—which is how we have been programmed at just about every level of experience—then we will assume that an attack occurred; therefore, a crime must have taken place. If we choose love, we'll find peace.

For example, crimes usually involve violence of some kind. This could be physical, emotional, sexual, verbal, or energetic violence. Perhaps a situation occurred in which someone crossed your personal boundary without your permission, physically attacking you or giving you an emotional stab or bruise. Your first instinct was probably to defend yourself, retaliate, or withdraw. Each of these instincts stems from a belief that the attack was real and that you are an individual person made up of an individual body. This is how you live in the world of humanity, also known as the world of duality, where crimes happen every day.

Once you were convinced that a crime occurred, the people involved automatically fit into predetermined roles. We have a group agreement for these roles, which span all cultures and socioeconomic levels around the globe. We call these roles "victim" and "perpetrator." Sometimes there is another role: "savior"—a third person who swoops in to (temporarily) save the day. For our forgiveness practice, we'll focus on the victim and perpetrator roles, because they take us directly into our emotions, and that's the place to go for deep healing.

In traditional forgiveness, we keep these roles intact and try to heal. We say to ourselves, "I'll just let bygones be bygones. I'll try to forgive and forget." Or "I'll let the passing of time heal my aching heart. It doesn't feel so bad anymore. I've forgiven him/her." Or "They had such a terrible childhood, they couldn't help themselves. I feel pity for them. I have forgiven."

In order to be free, we need to enlarge and change what it means to forgive. Complementing the teachings of *A Course in Miracles (ACIM)*, Ho'oponopono (a Hawaiian form of forgiveness practice), and Radical Forgiveness (a healing technology initiated by Colin Tipping), we can use a philosophy that ultimately throws out the victim and perpetrator roles altogether. We expand our thinking and feeling to include all beings as equal, eternal, and holy. We can then experience a sense of peace that is never possible when we identify ourselves or others as victims or perpetrators. This peace is available to us only when we relax into the world of divine truth, where the grace of Spirit envelops us all.

The catch here is that we can't gloss over the knots of constriction and pain that we made in our emotional bodies when the upsetting events in our lives occurred. Especially when we were children, we didn't have the emotional maturity to separate ourselves from our parents, peers, and teachers. We didn't understand the impact of the pain they were carrying when it was projected onto us. We dutifully took on the legacy of their trauma and have done so for untold generations, just as I did when I felt attacked by Sal, my dance teacher. (You'll find out more about that in the next section.) And the thing is, we'll keep on projecting this mess onto our children, and they to their children, unless we stop the momentum. This is the most important stand we can take in life: we can say, "This pain stops with me."

> *To transform energies, we must experience*
> *them totally, working through them and*
> *forgiving them, which means seeing*
> *the perfection in them.*
> —COLIN TIPPING, *RADICAL FORGIVENESS*

I never ask anyone to forgive right away, or within any time frame at all. We all forgive when we're ready. That said, almost all of us have wounds that need to heal. And by saying that we need to heal, I don't mean that we are broken. We're not. But to truly feel peace directly, we can't skip over the work that is needed to release this pain from our minds, hearts, and bodies. That is the blessing of forgiveness: it takes us from isolation, fear, and pain all the way to deep inner peace. As we will see, forgiveness can touch our lives on many levels, from our physiology to our gender, culture, personal history, and family lineage. It reaches all the way to the earth's ecosystem, opening a path toward new health for every living thing.

When you engage in the work of forgiveness, you aren't trying to fix yourself, another person, or a situation. Forgiveness is the *inner* work we do to increase our experience of freedom. It brings us consciously into the world of oneness and divine truth. In the world of duality where we live as individuals, we also need accountability and self-responsibility, systems of justice, mediation, reconciliation, treatment programs, jails, and halfway houses. This is the *outer* work of living together in an unenlightened society. These inner and outer levels are connected, yet distinct.

With forgiveness, you aren't looking for justice in order to right an injustice. You're not a savior or a victim or a perpetrator—those are roles *you* constructed. You aren't bound by them, and neither is anyone else.

What a relief.

By following the steps outlined in this book, you will simply witness what you're carrying from the past, learn from it, and let it go. You will release the need to blame, shame, or take revenge on anyone—including yourself. This release will open up passageways that were blocked, perhaps for your entire life up until now. This means that all the love and wisdom of the divine will be available for you, now that you've ended your stormy romance with grievances.

With forgiveness, however you imagine God to be, you'll bring Him, Her, or a wondrous, ineffable Pure Awareness even deeper into your experience. Whatever religion supports you with a loving, limitless, openhearted experience is helpful here as well, but you don't need a religion. In fact, your past religious training may just get in your way, so open yourself to other possibilities if the old ones don't feel kind or welcoming. If you don't have a specific name for the divine, you can use the Holy Spirit, Great Spirit, Higher Power, the Goddess, or the power and beauty of nature. Names don't matter as long as your God-force is loving and compassionate.

Once you complete the process, the doorways of your inner meridians will open. You'll tap into an experience of true peace, which is to live inside miracles themselves. Life just doesn't get any better than that.

Forgiveness Is Not Psychotherapy

Traditional psychotherapy tends to make a religion out of telling the story, sometimes spending years dissecting every detail. Yet patients often remain within the safe zone of repeating the level and depth of emotion that is familiar to them. Unless the therapist is working with spiritual principles and encourages release into divine love, all the patient's stories, themes, and emotions remain with him or her. They may change and become more tolerable, but they are not healed. This is a fundamental distinction between forgiveness and traditional psychotherapy. The raw material of the human being overwhelmed by pain is the starting point for both. The end result is very different.

In most (but not all) psychotherapy, the story of the sickness or injustice is the main event, and the emotions attached become the object of study. In our forgiveness process, we witness our stories with compassion, but we don't hold on to them. We offer them up in prayer to the Holy One for divine healing. This is what many people do in church or at their temple or mosque. Some have deep, spontaneous healings, helping them connect with God within a religious context. Widening the sphere of possibility and opening it up to everyone, the river of divine love takes you downstream, giving you a specific, descriptive map of the logjams in your mind, a way to open the flow with forgiveness, and a direct channel to the ocean of universal peace.

An Example of What I'm Talking About

I had an experience that describes what I mean by forgiveness. It happened during yoga class, but it could have happened anywhere and come out the same way. The event included all the aspects, or levels (physical, emotional, mental, and spiritual), of my humanness *and* my divinity.

I was breathing into a pose that's always been tough for me. It's called *supta virasana*—a reclining pose that really stretches the knees. I was lying there, tuning in to my knees, and realized that my left knee was complaining loudly. I also realized that I'd had at least two big injuries to that knee. Lying on my yoga mat, I began to explore what might be going on in there. I wondered, could it be that my knee was acting as a reservoir for some of my unfinished emotional business?

I remembered the most recent injury: a skiing accident. I brought into my consciousness the most emotionally difficult thing about the accident, which wasn't the physical pain but the feeling of being trapped, controlled, and curtailed in my movement. The accident happened when I was in a major life transition, and I felt absolutely helpless, out of control, and demoralized by the fact that I couldn't move my body with its usual power and ease.

Then I went further back in time to the first incident, which happened when I was about nine years old. I wanted to see if the emotions I felt during the skiing accident were similar to the ones I had felt as a child. I wanted to release the sensations and feelings that were coming up, and let them out of my body.

Still breathing in *supta virasana* (or "awkward pose," as I call it), I allowed the memory to surface from my childhood as a nine-year-old. I was in ballet class, and my teacher (an irascible guy named Sal) came over to adjust my body. My left leg was up on the ballet barre in a stretching position. "Straighten your knee!" he growled and pushed down forcefully on my left knee. At that moment—decades later, lying on my mat in yoga class—I realized that I had really felt *attacked* by Sal. Rather than pushing on my thigh, he had pushed directly on my knee joint, injuring it and bringing lots of pain to my body. He also dumped a load of his personal unhappiness and dissatisfaction on me in that moment, and because I didn't understand what was happening, I took it on. This brought pain to my heart and mind as well.

I began to let all the emotions connected with both incidents rise up and out of my body and mind in a wave. Right there in the yoga studio, I wept in silence as I allowed the release. I was completely aware of what I was doing: I was making a choice to open an inner gate to that reservoir in order to release the pent-up anger, frustration, helplessness, indignation, bewilderment, and pain that I had stored inside my left knee. Each emotion came to the surface of my consciousness for review before it left my body through the open gate. In addition to my personal pain about the issues involved, I also began to feel Sal's pain, frustration, and bewilderment. Everything that came into my awareness was released, flowing out of my body on a wave of breath and compassion. This was a conscious offering to the divine in me, to that essence that gives me life.

As I followed my emotions, the tears stopped. Continuing with conscious breathing, I began to tune in to all the ways that Sal and I were very similar at that time in our lives. We each had an unhappy home life, stressful circumstances we didn't know how to handle, lots of suppressed misery, and no conscious way to release it. We shared all this, and we had no spiritual support, no way to heal ourselves or shed this burden. I began to send compassion, love, and care to Sal and my nine-year-old self. And as I did this, I saw in my mind's eye an image of Sal as he released the pressure on my left knee joint. I was now free to move!

What happened next astonished me. As I watched this movie in my mind, still breathing in the reclining "awkward pose," Sal and I began to dance in the ballet studio. We moved with fluidity, grace, and technical elegance. As if flying or dancing in a dream (which, in a way, we were), we glided across the floor together in blissful harmony with ourselves, each other, and the mysterious choreography that flowed effortlessly through us. We could make the highest jumps (what fun!) and turn, turn, turn in multiple pirouettes (oh yeah!). The moment I tried to analyze what was happening, the dancing would literally slow down, giving me direct feedback on how much I could interfere with the process if I wanted to. But I didn't want to, so I relaxed out of my mind and just let the dancing happen. Sal and I moved in freedom, perfectly in tandem, just like Olympic ice skaters. It was glorious.

Back in the yoga studio, the rest of the class was moving on. I took my time, letting myself be out of sync with the rhythm of the class. I needed to continue with my inner momentum, trusting that everything was unfolding perfectly. Feeling so much joy and openness in my body, I gave myself some time simply to enjoy the sensations and the freedom that came from releasing old memories out of my body, heart, and mind. We all moved into the final resting pose, called *savasana* (which looks like—and felt like—"saves Ana"), and I consciously breathed new light into the cells that had just let go of all that fear and tension. By drinking in the grace of God-consciousness, I replaced the old constriction with new vitality and life force. I ended the class with prayers of deep gratitude and inner peace. I had chosen a new moment for myself and my life's direction. In making the literal and figurative change from one old body to another new one, I welcomed a whole fresh chapter of possibility into my life. I had no idea where this would take me, and I really didn't care. I knew in my bones it would be good.

Connecting Emotional Release
with Forgiveness

In the story about Sal and my injured knee, it's pretty clear that I released a lot of emotion out of my body and that I felt a lot better once that wave of feeling had washed through me. But what does this really have to do with forgiveness?

Almost all of us have "knots" of old emotional pain that we've parked in different spots in our bodies until we're ready to release them. These knots are connected to stories, much like the spot in my knee was connected to Sal and the ballet class. When I decided to delve into my emotional reservoir, I did it in a specific way and used some of the specific steps that make up a process of forgiveness. In this book, you'll learn these same steps, so you can use them anytime, anywhere. Using the Sal story as an example, let's review what I did, and how the process linked me to an experience of forgiveness and freedom.

1. Since I was in a yoga class, I was already in a sincere place of spiritual opening.

2. I tuned in to the spot in my body that wanted my attention: my knee.

3. I slowed down and began listening to it.

4. With honesty, openness, and willingness (H.O.W.), I traced the pain back to the original crime scene,

uncovering the victim (me) and the perpetrator (Sal).

5. I allowed the emotions I'd bottled up in that spot to come out, using my breath and saying yes to tears. I gave all my pain to Spirit, and let Spirit do the healing.

6. I found a connection between myself and Sal and realized that we were not so different—we were very similar, actually. I felt Sal release his pressure on my knee, and the roles of victim and perpetrator melted away. I sensed the equality between us. At this point, I was traveling across the bridge of forgiveness.

7. I expanded the sense of connection I felt with Sal, which enabled us to begin to play together in my mind's eye, in a creative way. As we danced together, I experienced waves of freedom and joy.

8. The "crime" disappeared, and with it, the pain in my knee and the fearful memory of being attacked. I received Sal and myself as divine beings living in the material world, and made room for this truth to flow in my life.

9. I opened up new pathways for life force and intuitive wisdom to flow into my mind, body, and emotions. I ended with a prayer of thanksgiving.

Forgiveness Is for Everyone

Whether or not you meditate or do hatha yoga, forgiveness is available to you anytime, anywhere, whenever you are ready for it. The following chapters of this book will outline in detail the steps you need to practice this forgiveness process, either on your own or with the help of a trusted counselor or friend. It isn't difficult or complicated. It just takes honesty, openness, willingness, and dedication.

You may find yourself incorporating other steps that you find helpful. I'll give you the basics, and you can add your own color and style. Use the words and phrases that work for you to describe your spirituality and life experience. If you don't connect with the names God or Creator, use Goddess, Great Spirit, Higher Power, All That Is, or whatever moves you. What matters most is the desire for truth that you bring to the dance of your awakening.

Saying YES to Tears

In this book, I share with you what a forgiveness path looks like from the real experiences of real human beings. When I began putting together some stories for this book, I recalled personal incidents and also included some experiences of my clients (whose names have been changed to protect their privacy). One day, when I was reading them over, I realized how often I talk about my tears. In case you're imagining that I'm always running around crying hysterically, I want to put this forgiveness path into perspective.

"What's up with this crazy crying woman?" you might ask. Well, I'm usually quite sunny in disposition. And as I take off each veil of suffering, I get even happier. Yet when sadness and fear come up for review and release during forgiveness, I find that tears really help me to cleanse and let go.

Deep letting go, while holding on to our trust in a Higher Power, is the foundation of this work; whatever helps me get into the space of truth inside my emotions is where I want to be. Often, some tears are involved. Sometimes they softly trickle. Occasionally, I really sob when it's a major, soul-reckoning release. At other times, I don't cry at all. My clients are the same: depending on the moment and the personality of the person, tears come and go. It's all part of the flow.

I mention this as a way of encouraging you to be open to your tears. There are no strict rules in this work, and each person has their own beautiful way of releasing when the time is right. So welcome the possibility of allowing yourself to cry, especially if you haven't been comfortable with your emotions in the past.

Tears cleanse us on many, many levels, from the most basic physical release (think of it as an orgasm for your emotions) to the most mystical spiritual planes.

Let go, let tears, let God.

Forgive and Be Free: The Steps

These are the steps we'll be exploring in part 2 of this book. A review of the entire process can be found in chapter 13.

1. **Create sacred space.** Use prayer or deep intention to begin.

2. **Tell your story.** What is the issue that's bothering you?

3. **Navigate your emotional body.** Find and describe any discomfort in your body, thoughts, and emotions.

4. **Embrace your fear with love.** With trust, open your perspective so you can approach your suffering with love. Expand compassion for everyone involved.

5. **Listen for hidden messages.** Find out what's underneath the story. Take responsibility for the messages of your ego.

6. **Release.** Let go of everything that feels painful about this situation. Let it out of your body/mind with breath and intention. Offer all of your suffering to Spirit for healing.

7. **Witness the changes.** Notice any physical, emotional, and mental changes in the way you feel after your release. Is your connection to Spirit different now?

8. **Learn the lessons.** What is the teaching here for your soul? Why did you need this experience to deepen your inner growth?

9. **Soul expansion.** Drink in light and vitality with your breath. Expand to include a bigger circle with your love.

10. **Emanate a new life.** Each moment of forgiveness increases your intuitive ability. Your life opens as you feel more and more peace, and share it with all of creation.

How to Use This Book

Becoming truly free through forgiveness is what this book is all about. It gives you a step-by-step process to follow, in addition to the psychological and spiritual foundation of forgiveness as a working philosophy and practice.

In part 1, you'll learn about the essential importance of your emotions to your forgiveness practice—scientifically, socially, and culturally. Emotions link all of us into one family, as we feel the ups and downs of human life together. Following the experiential steps in part 2, you'll take an honest look at your human experience and soul patterns. From deep within, you'll pull forth a sincere willingness to release your grip on suffering and reach for trust in something bigger—a universal, loving force—that can accept and celebrate all of you. You will see that accepting yourself as you are—grimy *and* exalted, challenged *and* wise—can become a daily practice and a new way of being. Love, life, and forgiveness are embracing you no matter how tumultuous your situation looks or feels.

When you're actually diving into your forgiveness session, it will take far less time than reading this entire book. To get the most out of the process, you'll want to be familiar with the steps, so I recommend the following guidelines:

1. **Read the whole book first.** Get a feel for the territory. As you go through the chapters, I suggest writing down your thoughts, feelings, ideas, and any memories that come up. Then you can review your writing when it comes time to do the work.

2. **Make your forgiveness lists.** If you want to do something before your session, you can make your forgiveness lists (see chapter 5, step 2). I recommend handwriting them instead of typing them on your computer. There's something about the kinetic experience of handwriting that plugs you in to your emotions. When you physically write a person's name on your list and look down to see your own handwriting, it triggers a personal response that will support your release.

3. **Print out the free downloads.** If you would like, print the free downloads from my website as you come to them or print them all at once. That way, they will be easily available to you when you are ready to try the full practice. Everything that's contained in the downloads is already in this book. The downloads are simply offered in digital format for your convenience.

4. **Review the steps.** Once you've finished the book, refresh your memory of the steps by reviewing the last chapter, which can serve as a cheat sheet to use during your forgiveness process.

5. **Decide how to structure your process.** Decide whether you want to try your forgiveness alone, with a friend, or with a trusted counselor. Use your intuition and do whatever feels most real, honest, and alive.

6. **Holding sacred space.** If you choose to do the process with a friend or counselor, he or she should ideally have also read this book in its entirety. He or she should be sincere enough to be interested in the work personally, not just because it's "your work." Make sure it is someone who already knows how to "hold sacred space" (which is described in detail in chapter 3). You can't teach the person how to hold space for you while you're doing your inner work. You'll just

get frustrated and may give yourself an excuse not to finish. Bad plan. Instead, seek out someone who is clear and uninvolved with your story. This person should have a strong spiritual (yet non-dogmatic) perspective, and be someone who can stay away from gossip and negativity. Make an agreement to keep everything confidential. This will help you trust and relax.

7. **Do the entire process.** Forgiveness is a sacred doorway, and you need to give it the respect it deserves, so don't do it halfway. If you do it alone, go through the steps at your own pace, and finish them all. If you have a support person, make sure he or she knows what's involved. If you do it with a friend and you decide to trade sessions, schedule them for different days. Go through the whole process without socializing. Staying in the sacred space will give you the spiritual strength and support you need.

8. **Create sacred space.** When it's time for your session, follow the guidelines in Chapter 3: Creating Sacred Space. Give yourself time, space, clarity, and respect so that you honor your practice in the most soulful way. This is a gift you give to yourself. No one else can give it to you. Doing this well mirrors your sincere desire to live your life well.

Soon, you'll look forward to creating a sacred space for many aspects of your life.

We've always lived in peace in the deepest part of our being, but since we can be under the mistaken impression that we're ultimately separate and alone, the notion of a "return" seems real to us. We need a path to walk if we're returning to freedom. This journey can be called forgiveness, or divine healing, or any of a thousand other names in as many languages. I am with you as we travel on, together in the light.

PART ONE

Chapter One

Your Emotional Life and the Benefits of Forgiveness

When you delve deep inside your forgiveness process, you won't be thinking about anything but releasing your pain and diving into divine love. Because there is no forgiveness without connecting with our feelings, I want to include some information about emotions as they are experienced by human beings—in our brains, hearts, and cells. We'll explore the universal ways in which our bodies make physical, emotional, and mental connections. You'll see how essential your emotions are and how they link you to everyone in our human family.

Please keep in mind that I'm not a scientist. I'm giving you the basics here. If you'd like to know more about this kind of information, please read, research, and explore to your heart's content. For now, absorb this material as a foundation for understanding your emotional life. The main thing to remember is the way your body works *with* your spirit to give you unlimited possibilities for inner experience.

We are NOT alone, nor do we function separately. The fascinating complexity of the universe is mirrored in our brains, emotions, and cells. Human beings have the capacity to feel joy and sadness, fear and wonder, and it binds us into the fabric of life. Seen another way, each one of us is a facet that makes the diamond of creation shine with brilliance.

What Are Emotions?

Emotions are sometimes called "energy in motion." There is always a physical component to an emotional experience: it FEELS like something in our bodies. Emotions link the *mental* process of concluding, assuming, opining, and theorizing about reality with our *physical* bodies through corresponding *feelings* of love, fear, joy, anxiety, apprehension, excitement, and much, much more.

In Western society, our mental and physical levels are often more readily accepted as "real" and "important." We tend to get uncomfortable when talking about emotions. We hear about the mind-body connection— but where is emotion, and where is Spirit? In our hearts? Well, yes and no. As recent science attests and ancient wisdom has known for millennia, we are one entity with many interwoven layers. They all act together in an elegant interlacing of ingredients. As we will see, there is no dividing line between mind and heart, body and soul. All is One.

Emotions and Your Brain

Did you know that your body is made up of *trillions* of cells, and that *you were born with billions of brain cells?* Even as a tiny baby, you came equipped with a sophisticated brain that helped you manage your survival. By the time you read this book, your billions of brain cells have done their work and then been replaced by billions more. Delicately balanced brain chemicals silently guide every moment of your day, and continue on into your dream life as well.

Your brain stem, cerebellum, and midbrain supervise everything from blood pressure and heart rate to coordinated movement, sleep cycles, sexual attraction, and appetite. In the limbic section of your brain, you process emotions and long-term memories. This is the part of the brain that you work with most closely as you learn to forgive. You must access your emotions and memories in order to forgive. You'll also need help from your cortex, which is sometimes called the "executive branch of the brain." The cortex regulates decision-making and making judgments about incoming information. The cortex helps you plan for the future and get clear about your life path.

Neurotransmitters are chemicals that regulate the electrical signals between your nerve cells and your brain. When you think a thought (sometimes consciously but most often subconsciously), your limbic system and cortex send neurotransmitters to flood your system, and you feel the sensations of a corresponding emotion in your body. For instance, depending on the type of emotion, your heart rate picks up or slows down, your muscles tense or relax, your heart feels open or shut down. If you watch yourself closely, you'll be able to notice the influence of neurotransmitters in your body and the people around you.

There are many different kinds of neurotransmitters. One of the most important for our work together is oxytocin, one of the "peace chemicals." When your brain secretes oxytocin, you feel relaxed, centered, and bonded with your loved ones. With plenty of oxytocin in your system, you feel openhearted and empathetic toward the needs of others. These peaceful feelings uplift your life and the world around you. They are a natural byproduct of forgiveness and opening to the sacredness of life.

Yet most of us don't feel peaceful all the time. In fact, many people have a kind of crisis mentality, which may not be conscious, but shows itself in chronic irritation, insomnia, depression, or aggression. Their adrenal glands secrete lots of cortisol, the hormone designed to help us survive in dangerous situations. Cortisol is known as the "fight or flight" hormone, and is released by the adrenal glands in response to stress.

If we suppress the pain and fear of traumatic childhood and life situations (i.e., our issues that have not yet been forgiven), high levels of cortisol can become a regular ingredient of our bloodstreams, instead of an occasional visitor. When we hold on to old suffering and don't let it go, chronic overloading of cortisol can weaken our immune systems, increase our blood pressure, and shut down our reproductive systems. Our bodies call out for our attention by getting anxious and sick. This is one of the many ways that our spiritual intelligence communicates with us as individuals—by showing us that chronic stress in our emotions and physical bodies needs to be explored, released, and healed.

Oxytocin and cortisol seem to be opposites, but both are necessary for a balanced physical life. Forgiveness of traumatic experiences (be they large or small) lowers our cortisol levels and regulates them toward health. By letting go and letting Spirit take our pain, we increase oxytocin levels and feel peace and bliss.

Emotions and Your Heart

Despite what we may have learned in grade school, it turns out that the human heart doesn't just pump blood. Scientific knowledge about the breadth and depth of the physical heart's importance to overall health expands every year. Scientists are finding correlations between heart rate, heart rhythm, neurotransmitters, emotions, and peacemaking. This is truly a fascinating area of study!

According to researchers at the Institute of Heart-Math, healthy heart flow results when we have positive emotions. Our hearts then come into coherence with the rest of our body and the world surrounding us. Coherence means that our systems are in "logical, orderly and harmonious connectedness between parts."[1] When we are in coherence, we can tap into our heart intelligence, which gives us profound experiences of awareness, understanding, and intuitive wisdom.

There's a link between heart coherence and forgiveness. You can have one without the other. For instance, you can feel peaceful without doing all of your forgiveness work—but *not* on a continuous basis. If

---

1. Institute of HeartMath, "Research FAQS: What Is Coherence and How Can I Increase Mine?" Accessed October 28, 2013, http://www.heartmath.org/faqs/research/research-faqs.html.

you haven't let go of all your past pain, you will have stuffed it into nooks and crannies in your physical, emotional, and mental bodies. As you'll see in later chapters, you can easily find your pain and release it by following the steps in the second section of this book.

Our hearts offer a wellspring of life while we experiment as souls residing in physical bodies. The heart is our temple, and can be treasured as a precious jewel within each person.

The heart sends its pulse in the form of a blood pressure wave to the rest of the body's systems. It also communicates biochemically by releasing atrial peptide, which slows the release of other stress hormones, such as cortisol. It produces the strongest electromagnetic field in the human body. Studies by the Institute of HeartMath have found that our hearts are so powerful, they radiate their energy into an electrical field that is shared through touch or close proximity with another person.[2] It turns out that we share our heart field with those around us, all the time.

Emotions run in a spectrum from the highest vibrations of joy and peace to low vibrations of guilt and shame, with many possible flavors in between.

---

2. Rollin McCraty, PhD, Mike Atkinson, Dana Tomasino, BA, and William A. Tiller, PhD, "The Electricity of Touch: Detection and Measurement of Cardiac Energy Exchange Between People," Institute of HeartMath, accessed October 28, 2013, http://www .heartmath.org/research/research-publications/electricity-of -touch.html.

When we feel anxiety and fear, our hearts contract. Our electrical circuits overload. Our ease of communication decreases, we can't think or hear clearly, and conflicts with others increase. When we're "off center," our heart rhythms become jagged and sharp. That's when we need to use our tools, such as prayer, willingness, conscious breathing, honesty, and forgiveness, in order to come back into balance.

Heart balance aligns our entire system, and it flows from feelings of inner peace, gratitude, and harmony. Studies show that positive feelings of appreciation result in the following:

- Improved performance and achievement
- More creativity and innovative problem-solving
- Better decision-making
- More flexibility in the way we think
- Improved memory
- Improved immunity to disease
- Improved hormonal balance
- Longer life span

When we feel appreciation and gratitude, we have high levels of oxytocin cascading from our brains to our nerve cells, a balanced heart rhythm, and all of the benefits of a good life, as described by the preceding list.[3]

HeartMath researchers have also found that there are actually more electrical connections from the *heart to the brain* than there are from the *brain to the heart*.[4] Our hearts have a deep, innate intelligence. When we feel out of balance, our hearts struggle to help out, but we must choose to realign ourselves with positive emotions to come into coherence. The expanded form of forgiveness offered in this book gives the precise alignment technique that's necessary for us to enjoy a life filled with heart intelligence, relaxation, and joy.

Emotions and Your Cells

As we have seen, brain impulses, specific neurotransmitters, and heart waves link the brain with the rest of the body, directly influencing how we respond or react in any situation. In addition, every cell in our body is a mini-receiver and transmitter that gives specific feedback to the whole.

---

3. Doc Childre and the Institute of HeartMath, "The Inside Story: Understanding the Power of Feelings," Institute of HeartMath (2002), accessed October 28, 2013, http://www.heartmath.org /free-services/downloads/the-inside-story.html?submenuheader =6.

4. Rollin McCraty, PhD, *The Energetic Heart e-Booklet: Bioelectromagnetic Interactions Within and Between People*, Institute of HeartMath, accessed October 28, 2013, http://store.heartmath .org/e-books/energetic-heart.

It turns out that deeply held questions and beliefs about life itself (such as who we are, whether it's safe to be here on Earth, our purpose, whether we can love and be loved, etc.) directly affect our health, down to the microscopic level of the cell.

As our cells first begin to form, we receive incoming information in utero, through the placenta. Our mother's thoughts, fears, joys, and beliefs come to us from her brain waves, heart rhythms, and hormones. We also tune in to our father's feelings and state of mind through hearing his voice before we are born.

Stress, diet, behavior, and toxins in the home all influence how our physical, emotional, and mental bodies form in the womb. This is nature's way of helping us to adjust ahead of time to the conditions we'll find once we pop out into the family. We adjust, and we also absorb all of the highs and lows of our family system.

Cells in the body are exquisitely sensitive to incoming information. Chemical reactions in our cells switch our genes on and off, depending upon how we relate to our environment. Research has determined that only 5 percent of babies are born with genetic defects. This means that 95 percent of us regulate our genes through our attitudes about life, not through physiology. Dr. Bruce Lipton, a pioneer in the field of epigenetics (the study of genes, whether they turn on and off, how much, and why), says, "You're not controlled by your genes, you're actually controlled by your perception of the environment."[5]

We're particularly influenced by what goes on in our original home, both before and after birth. According to Dr. Lipton, scientists have found that during the first six years of life, a child's EEG brain activity is "operating in a hypnotic trance state, so that whatever the child is learning is being downloaded into the *subconscious* mind. The subconscious mind habitually plays back these programs."[6]

Choices made later in life influence our health as well. Identical twins, for instance, don't always develop the same illnesses, even though they share identical genes. Over time, epigenetic differences between them accumulate, especially when their lifestyles differ. One twin with a healthy lifestyle and peaceful thoughts may not develop the heart disease or cancer that the alcoholic, depressed, or overweight twin does. Drinking, smoking, eating, and anxiety all influence our state of health. We inherit our genome (the genes themselves), but we can alter our epigenome (chemical instructions to the genes). We can rewrite the physiological instructions in our bodies through forgiveness and other healing

5. Dr. Bruce Lipton, *The New Biology: Where Mind and Matter Meet,* video, accessed October 28, 2013, http://www.youtube.com/watch?v=HVECAlT4AXY.

6. Dr. Bruce Lipton, *The Wisdom of Your Cells: How Your Beliefs Control Your Biology* (Boulder: Sounds True, 2006), Audio CD, Part One.

practices, changing the course of life for ourselves and future generations. This is why forgiveness and all releasing and healing techniques are so important. For health and deep peace, we must choose to let go of the pain in our personal and family history, right out of our cell walls.

Studies have found that it's not the nucleus that is the command center of each cell. Instead, the *cell membrane* guides how and when the cell receives nutrients and information.[7] The cell membrane scans its environment through protein receptor sites. When it finds appropriate incoming data, channels open up to receive nutrients. The channels also clean the cell by opening to flush out waste.

Receptors on the cell membranes respond not only to physical stimuli but also to energetic information. If we inherited a subconscious belief from our parents that the world is unsafe, for instance, we feel fear, and then we experience life as being fearful. Like the rest of our body, our cells function in crisis mode, which clogs the cell membranes with debris. Just like our brain, our cells can't think straight, can't respond efficiently to stimuli, and make mistakes about incoming information. Feeling fear then becomes a precursor

---

7. Dr. Bruce Lipton, *The Biology of Belief: Unleashing the Power of Consciousness, Matter and Miracles* (Santa Rosa, CA: Mountain of Love/Elite Books, 2005), pp. 66–76.

for physical disease, and incapacitates our ability to feel joy.

In my family, for example, my parents had a girl and a boy before I was born. They felt complete with having children. Then, one day, five-year-old Stevie had a bad headache. To their horror, my parents discovered he had an inoperable brain tumor. And even though my father was a doctor, he was helpless to defend his child against this invader. Stevie died within one month of the diagnosis. My sister was left to fend for herself emotionally, as the whole family was shattered by this tragedy.

Within two months of Stevie's death, I was conceived. Perhaps having a new baby was my parents' way of handling their grief. In the 1960s, conventional wisdom supported having another baby right away. Apparently, both my grandmother and aunt advised my mother to get pregnant as soon as possible, in order to fill the gaping hole of sorrow in the family.

My mother was still in shock. I grew in her belly, receiving all of her thoughts and feelings, and when I was born, I entered into a family whose very foundation had been tremendously shaken. In addition, I was a girl, not a boy, and although my father denied that it mattered, it's possible he felt profoundly disappointed not to be given another son.

To complicate matters, Stevie's death may have triggered a cataclysmic amplification of my mother's mental illness. Great trauma can sometimes do that. So from the time that I was growing my body in the womb or shortly thereafter, my mother began to lose her mind (more about that later).

To this day, I continue to discover how much this sequence of events affected my life. I can vividly see and feel some of my *samskaras,* as the Hindus call them. These are the imprints or impressions of earlier events that influence the subconscious mind. Specific health problems, such as debilitating headaches, can be linked to my position in the family—and how I perceived it. I realized that one of my soul themes is to find joy, because I incarnated into a pool of grief. Another theme is to let go of fixing everyone's problems, because it's possible that I was conceived to relieve my family members of their despair.

My story is an example of how environmental factors *and* genetics influence a lifetime. Stop a minute to review what was happening in your family when your mother was pregnant with you. You may not know much of the story, but you can feel into your intuitive perception of gestation and birth. Was your mother happy, healthy, and excited about your arrival? Was your father present and supportive? Did the family have shelter and food on the table? What stresses impacted your parents as they waited for you?

All these things are ingredients in the family soup. When you were born, you added your soul flavors, but you also took on the subconscious belief systems of the family. Only later on in life can you consciously decide which aspects you'd like to keep and which you'd like to release and forgive for better sanity and health.

As Candace Pert, a noted neuroscientist, stated: "Intelligence is in every cell of your body. The mind is not confined to the space above the neck. The mind is throughout the brain and body."[8] I'd add that the kind of intelligence that Dr. Pert is talking about is really Spirit in action. It can be completely loving—if we let it in by forgiving, releasing, and receiving our soul lessons.

The Medical Benefits of Forgiveness

HeartMath's findings mirror the benefits of traditional forgiveness as published by the Mayo Clinic, a leading research center and medical clinic in the United States. Combining findings from scientific and medical studies, Mayo clinicians found consistent health and social benefits of forgiveness, including the following:[9]

---

8. Candace Pert, PhD, on the program "Healing and the Mind," with Bill Moyers, video, accessed October 28, 2013, http://www .youtube.com/watch?v=yw0qxXQkals.

9. Mayo Clinic staff, "Forgiveness: Letting Go of Grudges and Bitterness," Mayo Foundation for Medical Education and Research (November 23, 2011), accessed October 28, 2013, http://www.mayoclinic.com/health/forgiveness/MH00131.

- Lower blood pressure
- Stress reduction
- Less hostility
- Better anger management skills
- Lower heart rate
- Lower risk of alcohol or substance abuse
- Fewer depression symptoms
- Fewer anxiety symptoms
- Reduction in chronic pain
- Increased immune response
- More friendships and healthier relationships
- Greater psychological, religious, or spiritual well-being
- Improved well-being

All these benefits describe a healthy, happy, connected person. Widening the reach of forgiveness beyond the traditional model, as we'll do together throughout this book, only increases these benefits by expanding our conscious experience of Spirit. Imagine if everyone on Earth learned to forgive! We'd uplift everyone on our planet in no time.

Chapter Two

Gender, Family, Culture, and Our Deep Need to Heal

When a baby is born, the first question everyone asks is, "What is it, a girl or a boy?" As newborns, we can't help but notice that everyone's interested in which kind of body we have. It seems to be the most important aspect of our arrival! As eternal souls touching down on the tarmac at Gaia station, we must think this is very odd. Welcome to Planet Earth, where your gender matters.

Right after birth, the adults wrap the tender young babe in a blue or pink blanket (or similar traditions for boys and girls in different cultures). From that moment on, social conditioning begins. We have no choice but to experience it and absorb it. This imprinting is part of the escapade of having a lifetime on Earth. It impacts each one of us on many levels of experience.

Your gender directly affects your emotional landscape. Whether you feel at home in your femininity/masculinity or not, either way, it influences you and the quality of your life.

I find this to be a vastly intriguing subject, mostly because it seems that males and females really do come from different planets. Finding common ground and learning about each other are crucial to deepening compassion and balancing our energy. I believe that each of us is growing toward a balance between yin and yang—i.e., feminine and masculine energies. That balance is unique to each person. Some will be more androgynous, some more "femme," some more "macho." It doesn't matter which category you may be in. What matters is that you feel totally at home inside, because you've found the peace of your true essence.

Because of the inevitable dictates of social conditioning (as well as physical factors), men and women handle emotions differently. Take a look at your fears, and you'll find some of them gathered around your belief system about gender. For example, boys and men are taught to be afraid of appearing stupid or weak.

Girls and women, on the other hand, are taught to fear looking ugly and old. Our egos hate a bad image!

The male role belief system (MRBS), as it's sometimes called, encourages toughness, individuality, and competitiveness. It supports men and boys in feeling anger or happiness, but not sadness or grief. On the flip side, the female role belief system teaches girls and women to exhibit nurturance, softness, and compassion. Females fit into most cultures when they show sadness and tears, but not anger or rage.

Everyone with an ego fears "losing face" and a sense of identity. This is because the ego's sole purpose is to make separation between me and you, us and them, inner and outer, human and God. For both men and women, when our emotional safety or physical survival seems to be threatened (whether it truly is or not), we can also be afraid of feeling the intensity of our emotions, of being exposed in front of others, and seeming vulnerable or unsure of ourselves. Anger, even when hidden, often covers our fear and sadness as we try to protect ourselves (and our social image) from pain and loss.

Can you relate? Take a look at how your body, your gender, and social expectations affect your emotions on a day-to-day basis. What you discover may astound you—this one goes really deep. Keep in touch with your feelings as they arise, noticing the influence of the "boy-girl thing" in your life. What do you find?

Bridging the Gender Chasm

Contact between men and women can be one of the murkiest channels of human connection. For many reasons, both human and spiritual, we have a hard time bridging the steep canyon that seems to separate us.

Spiritually, many of our soul themes emerge through connection with our parents, especially with the opposite-sex parent. Traumatic episodes that occur early in our childhood or teen years link to fearful beliefs and attitudes about life. In addition, the lineage of family attitudes about what makes a "real man" and a "real woman" gives us plenty of material to strengthen (or derail) our spiritual awakening.

On a physical level, research shows that males and females function quite differently from each other.[10] Brain studies show that male and female brains at rest are completely dissimilar. The male brain, while resting, will power down more completely in the cortex and midbrain. That's why men like to have a "man cave" to go to, in order to recharge. When stressed, men produce more testosterone, which increases a tendency toward aggression. They interrupt more, which can lead to arguments and escalating conflicts.

Women, on the other hand, use their brains with more range in both hemispheres, even when at rest.

---

10. Michael Gurian, "Authors@Google: Michael Gurian," (September 10, 2008), video, accessed October 28, 2013, http://www.youtube.com/watch?v=jUMqArkEuW0.

Female bodies tend toward higher production of serotonin, oxytocin, estrogen, and progesterone, which are sometimes known as "consensus-building" or "bonding" chemicals. Since women bear children (and have to bear the crying and pooping of babies) and are the first teachers of each new generation, it makes sense that women use more of their brains while listening, are more verbally fluent, and are more comfortable with intimacy than men.

Research shows that one in five women and one in seven men have "bridge brains," which enables these folks to embody both male and female traits more easily. If you are a bridge-brain person, you might be verbally proficient *as well as* direct in your communication style, or have great spatial aptitude (usually a male trait) *and* be emotionally aware. A bridge-brain person gets the best of both worlds, but may only exhibit bridge tendencies in specific areas of life, like work or play. At home, the same person can return to a more feminine or masculine brain personality.

There are social drawbacks to being a bridge brain, however. Males may not fit into the "real man" box that mass culture expects. They may be more feminine in their interests or appearance, and run the risk of being bullied and misunderstood. (More forgiveness opportunities! They're everywhere…) Females with bridge brains may not enjoy "girl culture" activities, such as shopping or interior decorating. If their communication style is strong and direct, they run the risk of being labeled "unfeeling," too "butch," or a "bitch." For everyone, including bridge-brain people, becoming comfortable in our own skin is the only way to be truly successful in a society that wants to stereotype and control us.

What I just wrote is not my opinion—it comes from brain research. This means that many arguments between men and women (with resulting emotional triggers and forgiveness opportunities) really do stem from the Mars-Venus divide. We often misunderstand each other because of our chemistry, our expectations, and our lack of good communication skills. Knowing this, we can have more compassion for each other, give our loved ones more space to be who they are, and not take things so personally! Your forgiveness practice will help with all of these things.

The puzzling mystery of the sexes shows up everywhere. When I taught peace education and violence prevention as a guest instructor at San Quentin Prison, the men always wanted me to talk about the way women think. In the classes, they discovered how their violent actions stemmed from being too rigid in believing the male role belief system (MRBS). Examples of the MRBS are familiar: "Toughen up." "Be a real man." "Don't cry." "Don't show your feelings, except anger. Anger's okay." "Be a provider." "Control your woman. Be violent if necessary."

When these men relied on their size and strength to overpower and control others, they lost their peace and became dangerous people. (We liked to point out that MRBS translates into "Mr. BS.") They'd absorbed a lot of MRBS throughout their lives, beginning in early childhood, but no one taught them about girls and women. It was inspiring to help the men learn to respect a woman as much as a man, listen to her opinions, and give her as much freedom as a man takes for granted.

The inmates were just as confused about what makes a woman tick as many men might be. To help them see what social conditioning for females is all about, my then-sixteen-year-old daughter and I drew up a list of many of the aspects of the female role belief system (FRBS). It was four pages long by the time we finished and included things like this: "Be young, cute, and pretty at all times." "Be smart, but not smarter than your man." "Be submissive so your man doesn't get angry." "Be nurturing to your family. Put their needs above your own." "Be embarrassed about your body."

I read our list to the guys in prison and eventually developed a seminar using their feedback. Together, we mapped out all of the assumptions and rules about being male and female in our society. We discussed what was acceptable and what wasn't. Sometimes there were cultural differences, but after teaching the seminar around the world, I've discovered that there are many,

many more overlapping commonalities than there are exceptions to the rules.

Whether you identify as straight, gay, or otherwise, what are your feelings about gender—your own and the "other" one? Have you examined your beliefs about stereotypes? Do you feel jaded or cynical because of past pain in your relationships? Do you protect yourself from intimacy? These questions will bring some areas needing forgiveness to the forefront of your awareness. Becoming more conscious of gender dynamics is essential for your healing journey.

Your Family Lineage

After you were born and the adults swaddled you in an appropriate blanket, you beheld your family. All the "good" and the "bad" in the family was actually a perfect mixture for your soul's growth. Every emotional and energetic connection your soul needed was contained within your family matrix.

In your family, you quickly learned all about emotions and relationships. You watched your mother and father interacting, as well as extended family, grandparents, and siblings. This is true whether or not your parents were physically living in your household. The soul essence of your parents was (and is) with you, even if they lived somewhere else, had another family, or died while you were young.

The family dynamic taught you whether or not it was okay to be loud, boisterous, and passionate, or quiet, introverted, and "polite." The cultures of your parents also touched the family, including the languages they spoke and the religions they held as sacred. You learned a lot from Mom, Dad, and everyone else who influenced your childhood.

Think about your household growing up. Recall the smells, the sounds, the taste of the food, and the feel of the house and neighborhood. How did your childhood home affect you? What emotions come up for you as you recall your childhood?

Many people experience joy at remembering a happy childhood. Others wince as they remember the confusion, dysfunction, fear, and pain of their early years. Whatever comes up for you—perhaps a mixture of a lot of things—make sure you give it respect. Give yourself time and space to explore feelings related to your youth. See if the same emotions often come up for you today. The emotional world you grew up in probably infuses your life now, and it will guide you in your forgiveness practice as you embark upon the steps outlined in part 2 of this book.

Emotional Tone or Vibration (Like a Musical Note)

Which emotional tones were most active in your child-hood home? Like music, emotional tones speak to your most tender, inner-heart places. For example, did your early home feel light, fun, and supportive, like a polka, Texas swing, or mariachi band? Or did it feel more like a heavy Wagner symphony or funeral march? Did the family music have a vibration of fear, silence, secrecy, joy, laughter, playfulness, worry, illness, depression, confusion, creativity, and/or ... what else?

Emotional music is with you now, in your adult life. Are you playing the same melody you heard as a child? If you had a tough childhood, don't despair. It's possible to strengthen your connection to the positive aspects of your early life. Forgiveness will show you the way.

Culture and the Collective Level of Feeling

The cultural stew that we're born into influences us from the moment we arrive. It adds flavors to the personal and relational concoctions we brew, deepening the aroma as time goes on. Our culture, or a mix of them, helps us relate to the wider human culture that's alive on Earth.

Merriam-Webster's Dictionary defines the word *culture* as

(a) the integrated pattern of human knowledge, belief, and behavior that depends upon the capacity for learning and transmitting knowledge to succeeding generations; and (b) the customary beliefs, social forms, and material traits of a racial, religious, or social group; also, the characteristic features of everyday existence (as diversions or a way of life) shared by people in a place or time.

In my classes, I've had the good fortune to teach people from a wide variety of cultural, national, and religious backgrounds. Peace education seminars take me to prisons, juvenile halls, schools, and conferences. Inmates sometimes come from neighborhoods and cultures I haven't had a lot of exposure to, and I like to ask them about it. We talk about what it's like to grow up African-American, poor, and from the ghetto in L.A.; or Sicilian-American, with brothers, uncles, and father in the "family business"; or Native American, angry, disillusioned, and rebellious; or white, poor, and barely sober, but without the emotional skills to handle jealousy and violence... the list goes on and on. Each person has a different mix to work with, which brings out his or her soul themes and areas of learning.

In an emotional empowerment class, students told about the impact of feeling like an outcast, ostracized from the culture of the majority. One described moving from a farm into town and being typecast as a "hillbilly" (complete with the shame of believing the bigotry of the "townfolk"—she felt bad about being a hillbilly for forty years!). Another talked about being seen as "the rich kid" in her town, even though her family didn't have a lot of money, because her father had a better education than most. She struggled with that label for a long time, too.

While teaching a restorative justice class at a juvenile hall, I got a firsthand look at the impacts of culture on our youth. Born in rural poverty, many of my students had parents who were between fifteen and seventeen years old at the time of their births, and some were already parents themselves. My students all experienced massive amounts of violence in their homes from day one. It seeped into their bones, their minds, and the way they felt about the world. Almost all of them felt that revenge was the best (and only) course of action to any affront, disagreement, or "disrespect." Steeped in a family stew of aggression, they took pride in showing off their gang affiliations, tattoos, and stories about earning their stripes to prove themselves to the other gang members.

Their pain throbbed in dull waves throughout the hall, coming out in laughter as well as tears. It was generational pain, carrying poverty, drugs, and violence in its wake. Many students were living with the horror of genocide, since they were of Native American descent. Others came from white and Latino backgrounds. All of them were bound for prison unless they made profound changes in the way they thought, acted, and felt about the world.

Fortunately, after a few weeks of testing me mercilessly, we grew to enjoy each other in a quirky sort of way. I taught them peace education, and they taught me patience and perseverance. I fell in love with every single one of them. Time will tell whether what they learned will stick, and whether they will make healthy choices in the future, but now they have a foundation for their path of forgiveness.

Another example of the effect of culture occurred in my family. My grandmother grew up as a poor, urban Jew. She lived in an immigrant ghetto in New York City when she was a small girl. Ghastly tenement fires were a common occurrence back then, and I'm sure she witnessed them or perhaps needed to escape from her own home when she was a child. Her fears never left her (i.e., she hadn't forgiven them), and they translated into worries about her family as she tried to protect us from the terrifying memories she had from childhood.

By the time I came along, we all lived in the suburbs. There were no tenements and very little risk of fire. Physically, our lives were much safer than what people endured in my grandmother's time, but the fear lived on, moving from Granny to my siblings and me. She always used to say to us, "Make sure you wear your pajamas at night, in case there's a fire!"

I grew up terribly afraid of an inferno that might erupt some night, any night, only recently realizing that my fear stemmed from generations-old thinking and memories. I kept this fear throughout my childhood, and finally grew out of that deep sense of night-time panic when I left my family home. Weird, huh? That's how culture and memories are passed down through the generations—non-rationally and based on fear and helplessness, joy and pride, and every emotion in between.

Take a moment to review the culture(s) with which you identify. Include your sense of patriotism and nationality, subcultures you belong to, and religious affiliation. Do you have any love-hate relationships with your culture(s)? Have you run away from one, and chosen to embrace another? Do you still nurture childhood memories that are linked to holidays, ceremonies, or attitudes you received from your family? How about the underlying culture of the country you were born in, or moved away from?

All of these things affect your emotional life, because every culture has unspoken rules about how to deal with emotions. The culture of your family, language, religious traditions (or lack of them), and subcultures of teen life or sexual identity form your sense of self on a very personal level. You may be carrying a lot of this around and don't even know it. Culture and all the assumptions, thoughts, and emotions that come with it infuse us, often subconsciously and from very early in our childhoods, making our lives rich and colorful. Culture is an amazing thing—hard to describe yet palpable in its impact.

As you explore the areas in your life that you'd like to forgive, keep your culture and gender in mind. When you uncover areas of pain or fear, check to see if any aspects of cultural or gender identity play a part in the story. They will appear as part of the set design that illustrates your current incarnation. Even if they seem harsh or unsupportive at first glance, they can be used to help you with your awakening.

I've found that the more I become aware of the many varieties of human experience bubbling up in my life, such as cultural and gender experiences, the more compassionate I can be when the same thing arises for someone else. When I realize that I've been conditioned since birth to think of myself in a certain, very limited way as a girl and woman, I can relax into feeling this truth for millions of women worldwide. When I tune in to the hardships of social indoctrination imposed on men and boys, I can turn away from anger and separation from them and embrace them as brothers instead. In truth, there's only one of us here. When we can really live from this simple reality, we find strength and love for each other that heals us and brings us peace.

Part Two
The Steps to Forgiveness and Freedom

Chapter Three

Step One—
Creating Sacred Space

When humans participate in ceremony,
they enter a sacred place.
Everything outside that space
shrivels in importance.
Time takes on a different dimension.
Emotions flow more freely.
The bodies of participants become filled
with the energy of life,
and this energy reaches out
and blesses the creation around them.

All is made new;
everything becomes sacred.
—Sun Bear, Chippewa author and spiritual leader

What Is Sacred Space?

Sacred space is actually with us, around us, and inside us always, but in our fast-paced society, we rarely notice it. Because we've been trained to see the external, material world as more real than our own inner life (and because we have acquiesced to this training), we need a mechanism to turn our focus around. Creating a sacred space is an integral part of consciously bringing forth and including the spiritual aspect of ourselves in our own healing. For without spirit, true healing doesn't exist.

According to Webster's New World Dictionary, the word *sacred* means "belonging to God; consecrated; holy." To create sacred space, then, means that we give divine meaning to the space within us and around us. We infuse it with holiness by extending holiness back to itself, acknowledging what Native Americans call the "sacred hoop"—the linking of the divine circle or spiral. In returning consciously to the peace of the Mystery, we bring both space and time back to the eternal. As an offering, we lay the whole of the three-dimensional world on the altar of Spirit. When this happens, we leave space and time, making room for miracles.

In our sacred space, we honor our healing, and we also ask for help. It's a humble, open place that we search for and find within ourselves. We aren't pleading with God, nor are we making demands; instead, we rest in patience and simplicity. We bring in holiness and our recognition of its central place in our lives. We can add nothing to it, because its very essence is wholeness, but we do consciously include our vital awareness in its mix. It's a place of surrender not because anything is wrong, but because we want to receive the blessings of the divine. Without surrender, there's no room within us to receive. To create sacred space is simply to rise into the holiness that is already here, always welcoming us home.

Why Create a Sacred Space?

There are many reasons why we choose to begin the process of forgiveness by creating a sacred space. Two of the most important have to do with two essential aspects of healing that accompany us during the entire process:

1. *We create a safe place to release into.* By making a sacred space, we enter a place we can trust, a safe place to lay our burdens down with finality. By creating an inner place to put the pain of the past, we trust that we can give our troubles and trauma to Spirit, finally and eternally. In doing this, we ask for the help and support

of angels, masters, and other divine energies who guide our awakening.

One of the difficult things about letting go of emotion is the fear that comes up about where to put it once we're done with it. In our minds, the world can seem to be a dangerous place. Lurking in the shadows may be a thought that tells us this: "You can't let go of that terror and pain. What would you do with it? Where would you put it? How can you trust that you won't hurt someone—even more than perhaps you already have—with the shrapnel and barbed wire and general toxicity of it all? Better just keep it inside and creatively paper-mâché a few layers of denial over it. That way, it'll stay hidden. That's how it *should* be."

Some techniques of emotional release involve elaborate visualizations of putting the pain into a balloon and then floating it away or putting it in a garbage can. These techniques can be helpful, and if they work for you, great! But if you're like me, your mind is tricky. It asks, "Where did the balloon go?" "Who took out the trash?"

This is where the grace that lives inside a sacred space comes in and saves the day, for us and for all beings everywhere. In the end, we must be willing to release the stories and imaginative conclusions we've come up with, and we need help at this point. It turns out that the place our souls can trust is a consciously created sacred space. This is why a sacred space is so essential to the work of forgiveness.

2. *We drink in, draw from, and gather strength, inspiration, wisdom, and support within the sacred space.* The grace of the sacred feeds us on all levels of our being: physical, emotional, mental, and spiritual. Sacred space is a place to *reach toward* for intuitive wisdom, vision, and revelation. In fact, there is no need to go outside this space for *anything.* It's all right here, and nothing is missing. We feed our souls with the sustenance of Spirit. Not only does this feel simply delicious, it also changes the neural networks we've engraved on our brains. Receiving from the sacred space rewires our brains, hearts, cells, and blood supply. By actively breathing in the intrinsic goodness of our divine nature, we change our inner reality and, in so doing, change and uplift our lives.

Sacred Space Is Not a Place

Sacred space doesn't have walls or a floor, and it definitely doesn't have a roof or ceiling. What I'm describing is more like a "sacred float" into a state of consciousness— the river's divine return to the primordial sea.

Sacred space isn't subject to the limitations of physical dimensions. It's also beyond whatever emotional and mental images we may entertain. It does have a loving, compassionate, and inclusive vibration, but it won't likely conform to our pictures of what it should look like or feel like. For instance, if we have an assumption that love always feels warm and fuzzy, we may become confused or reactive when love comes to us with its full, intense, fiery truth. Or if we think being with God is something we have to "do," we may feel uncomfortable or lost when a quiet voice inside us tells us to just *be*. Here we receive yet another invitation to let go of the shore and go back to floating in innocence, even if we have no idea what that's really like, or who or what is there to support us.

Trust

As you gain more practice with welcoming holiness into your life, you'll trust its gentle power more and more. Trust is a big part of creating a sacred space, because the sacred—for most of us, anyway—is invisible. So we reach into a vast, formless field where everyone, no matter who they are or what they've done, is allowed to plug in. (In fact, we're already plugged in—it's just that most of us have forgotten.) Access for all is part of the truth of it. That means you and I are automatically included. So, no more excuses—time to dive in!

Slowing Down

The first step in creating a sacred space is a simple one: we must slow down. After all, we're preparing to do some deep healing work within ourselves, and we need to acknowledge this and give it the respect it merits. If we're still racing about in mundane activity and giving full rein to our "monkey mind," which jumps and swings constantly from one thought to the next, we can't very well settle into the sacred nature of our healing.

Slowing down with deep awareness has its rewards:

- We stop running away from discomfort, thus bringing relief from hiding and a return to dignity and self-respect.
- We build our "inner muscles" for further exploration, by using intention, focus, and determination.
- We witness the ego in action and learn how it works, so we can recognize it in the future in all its various guises and camouflage.
- We get the reward of hearing the voice of our emotional body—what it needs, the wisdom it has for us, and how we've felt about ourselves and others (perhaps for most of our lives).
- We receive the blessing of our intuitive voice, which only speaks to us from the Now moment, sometimes called "the holy instant."

I once had a client named Sherry, a very conscious and beautiful woman. She had traveled to India, did yoga, and had eyes deep with wisdom. She understood the value of forgiveness. But she was addicted to doing, playing, and being social. For her, the hardest part of her spiritual path was to get herself to slo-o-o-ow do-o-o-own and respect the work. It was as if she had brought most of her current gifts with her from a past life and, meanwhile, kept dawdling during this one.

Sherry knew she had to quit the "fun dance," because it just wasn't all that fun anymore. As she got older, the play looked more forced, and her inner pain was catching up with her. Her biggest hurdle was surrender, not only to actually feeling the pain and releasing it, but also to giving herself the time and space to begin her journey.

When things got bad enough, she would call me and we would have a session. I became the space holder that she knew she could trust. Her next step spiritually, though, was to do the work on her own.

It's clear that my job isn't to become your (or anyone else's) crutch. On the contrary, my job is to guide you along the path, teach you some steps and practices, and then empower you to slow down, tune in, and become centered on your own, anytime and all the time.

Exercise for Slowing Down

Here are some helpful suggestions for slowing down.

Sit down and get comfortable. Keep your spine straight rather than slouching, and feel the "tube of light" that goes through the center of your body. Take a few long, slow, deep breaths and invite yourself to be completely, thoroughly PRESENT IN THIS MOMENT.

Slow the activity of your mind by reminding yourself of your commitment to bring truth to yourself through this healing work. Slow down and let yourself feel the tender places inside you. Feel the emotions connected with how much you want to heal and how willing you are to do whatever it takes to experience this healing. Throughout your forgiveness session, continue to draw on these feelings of sincerity and willingness, remembering that emotions are both the path and the doorway to forgiveness. Breathe and relax into the moment as much as you can, and continue for as long as you'd like.

Ways to Create Your Sacred Space

Make a clear place to work. Turn off the TV, phone (and don't forget the cell phone), fax, computer, and the busyness of the day. If you have children, arrange a time and place for them to be happily occupied, so you won't be interrupted. Go to your holiest place—in your home, in nature, or wherever you can most easily focus and concentrate on your intentions.

Once you've decided on the place to do your inner work, clear out any clutter there. This doesn't mean you need to clean the house from top to bottom, but you will want to surround yourself with beauty, clarity, and spaciousness. So if you're in your bedroom, straighten up a bit. If you're outside, make a comfortable, clean place to sit. By doing this, you're telling yourself that you want dignity and order in your outer space, which will mirror the clarity you are going to bring forth from deep within you. As always, what happens on the inside is the main event, so don't get lost in making the outer scene perfect. Just give it some attention and some love. You are welcoming the grace of Spirit into your life, into your mind, and into your body and blood, so you want to respect it with all the reverence of your heart.

I have a few places in my home where I go for prayer and inner work. One has a beautiful view of Mount Shasta, in all of its snow-capped splendor; one has a lovely altar; and one is outside. Depending on my mood and the weather, I just go to whichever spot feels most welcoming to me at the moment. It's a wonderful practice to develop sanctuaries in your home or somewhere nearby. It doesn't require money or even much time. It just takes intention to make an altar, which is simply a symbol of the clarity and peace you want to experience within yourself.

If you've never made an altar, you can have fun experimenting with what feels best to your heart. Even if you have an existing altar in your home, give it attention and switch things around every now and then. If you have flowers, keep them fresh and nice. Dried flowers are beautiful, too.

With openness and willingness, you will make a sanctified place that reflects what you love. What it looks like will depend on your personality and background. Generally, simple is best. You can add candles, photos of teachers and saints, shells and other nature items—anything that brings your attention back to the sacredness of life. The point is to make quality time and space for solitude and healing.

Prayer as an Act of Connection

Prayer is one of the best tools we have in the awakening process. It's a way to reach out of and beyond our familiar psychic environment and consciously invite more love and peace into our lives. When we pray, we sometimes ask for help, and in doing so we're admitting that we can't go any further without connecting to our divine source. This brings humility to our hearts and minds, and humility is always a great place to begin.

To use prayer is to make a statement to ourselves and to the Oneness that gives us life. In our constant conversation with Source, we say: "Okay, I admit it: you created me. I didn't create myself. I made my situation, but not my soul. So I need to return. I need to go back home, pulling myself hand over hand on this tether of life, toward the center of all that is. I do this with prayer. Please help me release all illusion and let go of whatever is false. Help me heal and come into truth."

With prayer, we invite support and intuitive wisdom into our lives. Even though we're speaking to the immensity of Divine Being, we don't need to request something from outside ourselves. Spirit is not an "other" to whom we must plead our case. It isn't a fearsome judge, and the angels and masters are not a jury. *God is a constantly available healing force of creative love,* and with prayer we consciously invite more of this force to enter into our mind, emotions, and body.

To Pray Is to Be Humble and Human

When you let yourself relax into the space of prayer, you join billions of people across the globe who pray *right now* in their own languages and cultures. There are countless prayers that have survived thousands of years, and many of them are just as compelling today as they were centuries ago when they were first spoken.

Prayer is a way of coming together with every other human being who has been grateful for the immense gift of life, or felt frail or afraid or in need of help in some way. I'm not suggesting that to pray is to be weak—not at all! Rather, when we take down our walls of pride and isolation, we can merge with the greater whole—and this is where our power lies.

To utter a prayer is to open ourselves to the healing, helpful force of infinite Being. It doesn't matter what language we speak or which names we use, or what happened or how we feel. Prayer is the great equalizer, because through it we agree to become humble and ready to learn. Through prayer we say yes to receiving specific teachings and realizations, and make clear the way to light, love, and wonder.

> *God speaks in the silence of the heart.*
> *Listening is the beginning of prayer.*
> —MOTHER TERESA

Your Prayer

Which aspects of pure essence do you want to invite into your forgiveness process? Embody them in your prayer. Send waves of intention out into the invisible realms to make a statement and an imprint on the stuff of life. For instance, if you want to invite honesty and willingness and healing, begin embodying these qualities inside yourself as you pray. For each quality that you want to experience, consciously bring it into your heart and mind as you speak.

If you'd like, add an invitation to masters, saints, and angels, asking them to join you in your sacred space. Later, you will call on them for support and courage. You'll all sit together in a council circle, and it will remind you that you are never alone in your awakening.

In this kind of work, prayer works best if it's spoken out loud. By speaking our prayers, we bring our intention all the way into the physical world. We don't hide out inside the imagined privacy of our minds but, rather, make a statement for anyone to hear (even if we're alone during the process). It's powerful to hear your own voice, and once you've said it out loud, you can't pretend the prayer never happened. It did, and it's real.

The following prayer is just one of the infinite possibilities in the world of prayer. I wholeheartedly encourage you to pray about whatever you are feeling in the moment rather than use existing prayers that you may have relied on in the past. It might feel a little strange at first, but try it anyway. It'll be worth it, because praying spontaneously demands creativity and vulnerability. It gets you out of your mind and into your heart, taking you precisely into the present moment. And after all, what else is there?

During your opening prayer, *fully commit to the reality that what you pray for will come to you* during the session. This prayer will be answered, because your willingness and sincerity will manifest it as you continue to explore the issues at hand. Open yourself to receive whatever you pray for. And don't get too caught up in preconceptions of how it's going to happen. Whatever comes out of your mouth will be the perfect thing, as long as it comes from your tender, open heart.

Beloved oneness,
Creator of all,
I open myself now to receive love's blessings.
I pray a prayer of honesty, openness, and willingness.

I pray a prayer of healing, humility, learning, and release.

I am willing to receive inspiration and instruction.

I am so grateful for life as it is right now.

I open within to include all of myself.

I include both the light and the dark,
the conscious and what has been unconscious.

May all of myself become known to me!

I invite the wise ones, the masters and angels, to be here in a divine circle of healing with me.

I give thanks for the assistance I receive.

I open myself to revelation and wisdom in the areas of _____.

I am blessed.

And so it is!

Chapter Four

Step Two— Telling the Story

After our prayer, we move on to step 2: telling the story. Here we reach into the human drama of our personal history in order to heal our memories of trauma, regret, and grief. Acknowledging our sole responsibility for whatever we find in our emotional landscape, we also take an honest look at how we've been holding the various situations that have been, and continue to be, painful for us.

When we enter step 2, we focus on forgiveness as a way to walk away from painful illusion, directing ourselves back to union with our Source. Forgiveness and the healing awareness of Spirit are always reliable guides, but to use the techniques efficiently (rather than just haphazardly, at random), we need a map that shows us where to navigate. Fortunately, the map is easy to locate because it lies within us, taking shape inside the stories of our lives.

When you chose to read this book, you probably had an emotional issue that was screaming louder than the others for your attention. You may decide to start with that issue, or you may want to go in slowly, beginning your journey with a minor upset, just to get a feel for the territory. Personally, I tend to enter intense emotional issues with gusto, but that doesn't always work best for everyone, so listen within and start with whatever conflict rises up out of the deep waters of your subconscious mind.

My Story, or How I Got into the Forgiveness Business[11]

Sometimes when I see friends with vibrant, healthy mothers, I marvel. One friend told me that she thinks of her mother as her best friend. I wonder, "What would it have been like to have had a mother who sur-

---

11. Adapted from Colin Tipping, Ana Holub, et al, "Forgiving My Beautiful, Wonderful, Crazy Mother," in *Why You Still Need to Forgive Your Parents, and How to Do It with Ease and Grace* (Atlanta, GA: Global 12 Publications, 2010), 65–83.

vived, who taught me the best ways to travel through life, who was sane and clear and able to support me?"

Yes, I marvel and wonder, and I can sometimes feel sad and left out. Growing up in my family wasn't easy. In fact, it felt pretty awful at times. But out of that turbulence came a powerful healing.

My Family Secret

I grew up in suburban New Jersey in the '60s and '70s with upwardly mobile, culturally Jewish parents who focused on education and success. My two sisters and I had our work cut out for us—we needed to conform and succeed. And while we were at it, we tried not to be too miserable. Our family shared good times, and the kids were physically well taken care of. Yet overall, our house vibrated with conflict and deception. We struggled to be a perfect suburban family, and we deceived ourselves and everyone else in the process.

Until my mother's death in 1985, she was a loving, creative, talented, and beautiful woman, as well as an accomplished pianist with a wonderful, artistic flair. She also was fearful, confused, confusing, giddy, depressed, silent, unstable, and massively inconsistent. Today a doctor would diagnose her with bipolar disorder, or manic-depressive disorder. As her child, I only knew I loved my mother, but I sensed something in our house was deeply and mysteriously wrong.

The split in my mother's mind was extreme and dangerous to her health. My entire family suffered along with her as we swung dizzily from love to anger, confidence to fear, and exuberance to panic. While her mood changes were fairly obvious, most of our swinging was done silently, almost entirely on interior, psychological levels, because we were all trying so hard to be a "normal, happy family."

We had a secret: Mom was depressed and had become unglued. We also had a bigger, unconscious secret: the whole family was crazy, but we were in deep denial. That dynamic was enough to make all of us run in five different directions, alone, confused, and without any help or spiritual guidance.

Living at my house felt surreal at times. As a child, I had the hardest time with "Double Mom." One mother was real—the loving, caring, tender one. The other mother was erratic, occasionally aggressive, often withdrawn, and definitely not to be trusted. I never knew which one would appear at any moment, which scared me and gave me nightmares. It seemed as if there were two people living inside my mother. One was kind and wonderful. The other was a group of malevolent phantoms who tortured me and my family. In my reveries, they would unzip my mother, take her out of her body, and replace her with their coldhearted presence. Then they'd zip her back up again, and no one could see the difference. Yet even as a little child, I could tell in an instant who was in residence inside of Mom. I always wondered where she went when the imposters took over her body, but I didn't know who to ask.

By the time I was ten or eleven, I had learned to sense from the smell of the molecules in my house whether this was a "high day" or a "low day." I'd walk in the door and literally sniff the air when I came home from school. When I was in high school, I realized that Mom's manic days could be worse than the despondent ones. My mother in a giddy mood seemed even more exasperating to me than when she felt depressed; she exhibited fewer inhibitions when she was "high," so I never knew what she'd do next. No matter which mood Mom was in, I just wanted to run—as fast as possible— and hide.

Depending on the day, or the hour, my mother could drastically change her ideas about life. For instance, one day she'd say, "You need a new winter coat. Let's go buy you a really nice, warm, fancy coat." On another day, however, I'd hear an indignant tirade from her about my "frivolous" behavior when I bought a slightly expensive shampoo. Frivolous was one of her favorite words—on the days when she didn't visit the mall on a manic buying spree.

To cope with the constantly changing vicissitudes at home, I worked hard to become "good." I thought being a good girl would bring me safety and acceptance. I got good grades, sang in the choir, and came home on time.

Later, when this didn't seem to bring me any success, I tried rebellion and teen angst. I broke the rules, snuck around at night, and sampled a variety of drugs for entertainment and self-medication. Though I tried to change "me" by changing my self-image, nothing could heal my heart or my problems at home.

Whether we wanted or agreed with them or not, my sisters and I had roles in society and in our family. My older sister played the part of the "smart one" and my younger sister the part of the "cute one." People sometimes called me the "pretty one," but I wasn't so sure.

"Am I beautiful?" I asked my mother more than once.

"Beautiful enough for all ordinary circumstances," she always replied.

I always wondered where she had gotten that line. I wanted her to say, "Yes, honey, you are beautiful in all ways, inside and out." My whole being wanted her love and approval. As my body changed at puberty, I also needed some guidance about how to handle the attention I got from boys and men, and her comment just seemed to hurt rather than help me. Like most teenagers, I felt vulnerable and confused about life. I knew, though, she was afraid that if she complimented me, my head would swell. She didn't trust my interior, and I didn't trust hers. We mirrored each other perfectly.

I Am Not My Mother

To top it off, by the time I became a teenager she often said to me, "You understand. Of all my daughters, you are the one who's most like me." In response to that remark, I developed chronic gastrointestinal distress. My father, a doctor, put me on medication, but after a few months I asked for therapy.

I just needed the therapist to tell me, "You are a different person than your mother. You don't sound like her at all." I felt so relieved when I heard those words.

"Thank God!" I thought to myself, "I am not *her*. I am not *that*."

Even though I loved my mother, she was driving me crazy. Sometimes my skin crawled when she was near me, and I backed away when she wanted a hug. Her neediness overwhelmed me at times. I just didn't know what to do, and no one else seemed to have any answers.

I felt so embarrassed when she'd meet my friends and say something really dotty, or forget their names or stare oddly into space. My friends loved her, because they saw her wonderful side. I loved her, too, but she was so unpredictable. I just wanted a mother I could lean on. Instead, she leaned on me. I didn't even know what it would be like to feel the comfort and guidance of a sane, healthy mother.

When it was time for me to attend college, I moved three thousand miles away to escape her and my father, who was a good, loving man but emotionally distant and absorbed in his work. I was suffocating on the East Coast with its intellectual pretensions, living in their New Jersey house and its hidden, unspoken anguish. I needed to get the hell out.

So I went to college on the wild West Coast. During this time, I rejected my family by joining another, experimental spiritual family. Yet I loved my biological family and felt terrible about myself for doing this. I had no idea where I fit in or who I was. Looking for solace in meditation and a spiritual teacher, I changed everything about myself (or so I thought) by taking another name, donating all my money and possessions to my new experimental family, and dropping out of school. I thought this would allow me to leave behind the discomfort of having a mother who was mentally ill. A part of me also felt a profound love for God and wanted a much deeper spiritual communion.

My parents had never fully been there for me even though they had tried. Mom seemed incapable of being an adult, and Dad had his hands full caring for her. No one was left to care for me, so I found a new tribe and a new life. I tried to leave my worries behind in New Jersey, letting the New Age in California guide my way.

At the age of twenty-three, I got pregnant. Even though the thought of becoming a mother scared me, I wanted to keep my baby. I had next to no money, little support from the father of the child, and my own father stopped speaking to me when I told him about the pregnancy. My mother, however, came to visit and gave me a maternity dress.

Her visit turned out to be a difficult one because her symptoms had progressed. She acted even more erratically, and I found myself vulnerable to the unpredictable rollercoaster of her moods. Despite this, her love truly touched me, and I felt grateful for her trust in me. Excited about the new baby, she did her best to bring some light into my world during this dark time.

About a month after her visit, I got the phone call.

My sister's unsteady voice told me our mother had committed suicide that day in the garage, by breathing the exhaust as she lay under the car. She'd also taken some sleeping pills to make sure she got to the other side. As I listened to my sister, everything seemed to slow down and my world appeared unreal, as if I'd entered a dream or suddenly been transported to another planet. I remember looking around the room, not being able to register where I lived, who I was, or what I felt. In shock, I hung up the phone and sat down on the couch. It was a long time before I could say a word.

A day later, in a daze, I got on a plane and flew home. All of us felt numb, adrift in the wreckage of Mom's deliberate death, barely able to function. I spoke at her funeral and remembered her beauty and her wonderful spirit. Round with child and devastated by grief, I wore the dress Mom gave me. I thought that blue denim tent dress represented her last gift to me, but I was wrong.

I Begin the Forgiveness Journey

In addition to being pregnant, I had no partner and no money at the time of my mother's death. I had friendships and my devotion to Spirit, which saved me, but this was a time when I really wanted the kind, sane, guiding spirit of a mother to help me.

I struggled to go on with life when my own mother had told me that creation, living, and survival were just not worth the effort. I wondered why she couldn't have stayed to help me with my new mothering. In addition, I found it almost impossible to cope with all the feelings that came up in me, including relief that her erratic behavior, fear, and sadness were gone.

A few weeks later, I gave birth to my incredible daughter and lavished my love upon her. I focused on life, not death, and tried to put my sadness aside. It took me eight years to open the emotional box into which I'd placed my grief, confusion, anger, and disillusionment. At that time, I attended a meditation retreat called the Enlightenment Intensive, which was modeled on the meditation practice done by Zen monks. At the retreat, I let myself crack open, and I felt the tender emotions I'd previously been afraid to feel. I cried and meditated, then cried, yelled, and meditated some more. My grief seemed endless, but eventually I felt clearer, more stable, and able to touch a bit more joy. From that day on, I began to have hope in the possibility of my own healing.

Maybe, on your own life journey, you've had the thought, "If I enter into those memories and feelings, I'll drop into a bottomless pit, and I'll never, ever be able to crawl out again. I'd better not go there."

I'd had that thought, too. I know exactly how it feels to stand at the edge of the pit, peering with dread into the oblivion that seems so dark and scary and mysterious. It took quite a bit of courage to allow myself to let go … and to trust that somehow I'd survive. I needed to fall, and I let myself take the plunge.

Another eight years went by. One day, I walked into a friend's house and spied *Radical Forgiveness: Making Room for the Miracle,* by Colin Tipping, perched on her coffee table. Attracted to its quirky title, I asked to borrow it. As I read the book, I discovered Radical Forgiveness as the missing link in my healing and in my work. Within a month, Colin Tipping came to Mount Shasta to offer a workshop, and I eagerly signed up to participate.

At the seminar, it was clear to me that a lot more layers existed for me to peel away before I could taste true freedom from my past. During one section, Colin turned up the music and we all yelled what we really felt; I couldn't even open my mouth. In fact, the rest of the group took a break outside while my workshop partner, Colin, and I sat together and did the exercise all over again until I could begin bellowing some serious sound. I was already a rebirther (a style of healing breathwork), but I found it incredibly difficult to put my feelings into specific words. I sincerely wanted to forgive, yet before Radical Forgiveness, I had no map and no specific steps to help me reach the inner peace I craved. At the workshop, I began to open up and learn about myself, feeling my emotions within a context of honesty and healing.

Discovering Memories and Puzzle Pieces

With Radical Forgiveness, we learn that whatever happens to us is not random, and even the toughest times have treasures buried within them. To find the gifts in my situation, I had to investigate my memories. I also needed to take a deep look at the interpretations and assumptions I'd made about my relationship with Mom. Only then could I separate truth from fiction.

I'd already discovered one memory during psychotherapy. When I was two, my mother raged at me. She was beginning to show signs of deepening psychological illness, and she had a two-year-old, a baby, and an older daughter to raise. She also was grieving the loss of my brother, Stevie, who had died a few years before. So, on that day (and maybe on many days), she really lost it. When I found this particular memory as an adult, I saw her standing over my crib, threatening me with a shoe in her upraised hand. Even though I don't think she actually hit me with the shoe, I was terrified.

I also remembered this: One night when I was about sixteen, my mother came into my bedroom. She was crying and seemed even more miserable than usual. She apologized for the attacks she had made upon me years earlier. At the time, I didn't think it had affected me. After all, I didn't even remember the incidents.

"Don't worry about it, Mom," I told her. "It's over."

Years later, however, after I learned about the power of forgiveness, I noticed how many of my anxieties and insecurities were connected to my life as a toddler. I found they were linked intimately with my emerging "victim story," or belief about the world, which often controlled me from the deep lake of my subconscious mind. My victim story said: "I must have done something horribly wrong and, therefore, I must be punished. No one loves me or will take care of me." This may seem like a perpetrator story, but I actually felt guilty, ashamed, and paranoid, as if at any moment a punitive God/Mother might pulverize me.

Like most children at the age of two, I thought the world revolved around me. I was just beginning to separate from my mother and form an ego. Perhaps because of the shoe incident and others like it, I became emotionally frozen in time. As I grew up, I made myself small and weak by bowing down to the power of my victim story. First, I compensated by being a "good girl," then switched tracks and became the black sheep of the family. All the while, I tried to find a self-identity that made sense to me.

I had a hard time making good decisions because I was haunted by a subconscious panic that I'd done something wrong and I'd be punished by some hateful, monster-like deity who wanted to destroy me. "You are a miserable sinner!" it screamed. I had to escape it at all costs.

A more recent piece of my life's puzzle came when I was in my mid-thirties. I'd married a wonderful man and settled into family life. During that time, I noticed that at about 10:00 in the morning, once my husband went to work and my daughter was at school, I'd start to feel anxious. After a while, I began questioning, "What is going on with me? Why am I so uptight? Why now and not an hour ago?"

Examining my feelings, I saw that when I was on my own for a few hours I felt tense, because I didn't have the early-morning distractions of taking care of everyone else. Tinged with a vague, uncomfortable feeling that I needed to do more and be more, I didn't feel adequate. I pushed myself to be better, to get more done, and to accomplish something of value.

A voice constantly nagged at me saying, "I must have done something horribly wrong." It also said, "I should have saved Mom from herself, but I didn't. I failed."

Looking back to my birth, I realized that this pattern had set itself from the very beginning of this lifetime. Since I was conceived just two months after my brother passed away, I subconsciously assumed I was supposed to sweeten my parents' pain by giving them new life. But I couldn't do it. I faltered in a mission I wasn't sure I really wanted and later rebelled against, and finally moved across the country to escape. With my mother's suicide, failure was inevitable. I couldn't save Mom, I couldn't save the world, and, until I radically forgave, I couldn't save myself.

My victim story caused me to feel tremendous anxiety and guilt just about all the time. Thanks to a buffering wall of denial, I scarcely realized this fact. Nonetheless, these emotions lurked maliciously under the surface of my waking consciousness.

Once I found Radical Forgiveness and began studying *A Course in Miracles,* my story emerged from the deep recesses of my subconscious even more completely. I began to see that my mother's illness symbolized the split in my own mind: life could be wonderful (caring Mom), then fall apart entirely (depressed, possessed Mom). I'd decided that good times couldn't be trusted. They'd just be followed by bad times. I felt trapped and helpless, because my victim story told me over and over I had failed. Unconsciously, I felt I'd done something terribly wrong, and no mother and no Creator would ever take care of me. The earth underneath me couldn't hold me, and I'd never be good enough to deserve God's love.

Gradually, as I slowly surfaced from my habit of denial, my life patterns became clear. I saw how over time I had taught myself to plan ahead for disaster, becoming a world-class worrier in the process. I married a man who didn't fret—at least out loud—and this brought the decibel level of my silent worries up to a dim roar inside my head. Caught in an invisible net of dread, nothing felt quite right. Even when life flowed easily, I worried that soon, misfortune would arrive.

Healing, Relief, and Inspiration from the Divine

To heal my experience with my mother, I needed to commit myself to the philosophy of forgiveness. I needed to slow down and take responsibility for all aspects of myself, including my relationship with abandonment and insanity. I had to release my ego's insistence upon duality and replace it with the truth about myself: I am lovable and I am love. To do this, I also needed to give myself a loving parent. I had to see myself as a loving and loved child of God.

By embracing all of my life experience—instead of desiring some of it and running from the rest—I began to see that my mother gave me love, a place to grow a physical body, nurturing, artistic talent, dance lessons, and so much more. She also gave me plenty of ways in which I could uncover my addiction to believing in my ego's voice as it nagged me with its victim stories. She offered me a vast number of opportunities to contend with my own feelings of fear and helplessness. As eternal souls, she and I helped each other in this lifetime—even if it looked like quite the opposite in the physical world.

For instance, I now see how my mother, as a focal point for my despair, anger, and blame, showed me how I refused to take responsibility for my emotional life. I'd kept most of this refusal unconscious and under thick layers of denial for years. I wasn't alone; this scenario describes a common strategy the ego uses to keep itself alive in most people. The mental places where I blamed myself and others were precisely the places where I hadn't yet forgiven. I could blame my mother because she'd attacked me when I was two years old, or because she had mental illness and it appeared she'd abandoned me. I could, and I have. It's easy. My mother didn't force me to keep telling my victim story to myself, though; she had passed on over twenty years prior. With the option of blame stripped away, I found myself alone with myself, my ego's voices, and my desire for change.

At this point, I clearly saw some of the lessons my soul came to Earth to learn. I already knew that the experience of living with a mother who suffered from manic-depressive disorder had affected my entire childhood. I couldn't count on her to "be there for me" and began (or, more accurately, continued) an internal story that the people I love will abandon me. Later, many other people I loved either left me or died. It seemed true: I was abandoned by those I cared for the most.

I began to contemplate how my mind had projected its fear-based thoughts upon the world. I felt so worried about being abandoned, yet I realized that on a soul level I may have attracted abandonment so I could learn from it and heal my misperception.

In lesson 350 of *A Course in Miracles*, I read, "What he is, is unaffected by his thoughts. But what he looks upon is their direct result." I was gently reminded that what I am is sacred, eternal, and whole, though my misunderstanding about reality caused grave suffering in my life.

I looked underneath that trusty blanket of denial and explored the specific spots where I had abandoned myself and others. *I asked myself where and when I'd been the crazy one, even if it was subtle or private or invisible to others.* I demanded that I see how I'd left my true nature and abandoned my connection to God.

This process humbled me and taught me compassion. Once I'd seen how much I'd embodied the same energies of fear as my mother had during her mental illness, I could no longer separate myself from her in the same familiar way. Yes, she had acted out in a spectacular way by taking her life, but I came to realize that dramatics don't matter much. Scale doesn't matter, either.

As souls, we either entertain our errors or we learn from them and heal them. Bringing myself to such a humble place taught me something more. Forgiveness felt great! I learned that humility is a good thing; it disarms the ego, and from that point new potential for health and wholeness comes to light.

Going Home

For me, forgiveness occurs when I realize I've abandoned love and truth and *I just want to go home*. I'm willing to do whatever it takes to see everyone involved as an equal child of God. I begin with prayer and honesty. Deep emotions follow and flow, loosening up all my misperceptions about myself and the world.

No matter what happened, no matter who was involved, whenever and wherever I was crazy—I exhale, forgive, and let go, as you will learn to do as you follow the steps in this book. If someone appeared to abandon me, I forgive and let go. If I appeared to abandon someone, I forgive myself and let go. Seeing when and where the world seems insane, I say, yes, I know. I forgive and let go. I go home to God. Forgiveness is the bridge, leading us directly to Spirit. Its heart medicine makes all things new.

Forgiveness showed me a way to heal the pain and anguish I felt about my mother's illness and death. I needed someone to lean on who could nurture me with soft strength and sound advice. Humbly, I called out, "Help!" and, crossing the bridge, took all fear and anger to the merciful heart of the Goddess. I let my pain and sadness go into her lap of love. It didn't happen all at once; this process took plenty of introspection, buckets of tears, volumes of spontaneous prayer, and a gradual shedding of layer upon layer of grief and memory. I called upon patience and the force of my will, combining them with the tender balm of her blessing.

I let the Divine Mother lead me to peace. She seems invisible, yet I've found that she is trustworthy.

Through forgiveness, I learned to find life's gifts and to embrace my mother just as she was, just as she is, a divine, eternal being of light ... just like me.

From my new perspective, I see my mother's life and death as just what she needed for her awakening. She pointed me toward the divine, and especially into the eternal care of the Divine Mother. With a huge sense of relief, I discovered that Spirit would never leave me, even if my earthly mother needed to pass on. I could finally be at peace with all the events that happened, and even better, see how they served me in ways my soul desired for my liberation.

Every day I learn more about my connection with my Source. *A Course in Miracles* tells us that reality is by its nature pure and loving. To meet it, we must match its love and purity of heart. That's all we need to do; the rest is already given. By releasing our sorrow and anger with forgiveness, we uncover the essence of self that lies patiently waiting. Spirit keeps the truth for us until we're ready to claim it as our own.

How ironic it is that I received such opposite messages about life during my childhood. My victim story convinced me that I'd done something horribly wrong and was abandoned by the ones I loved, and that insanity was so terrifying I had to run away. At the altar of divine love, I realize none of this is true. It was never true. In fact, as an eternal being, I haven't done anything wrong. I'm not abandoned or crazy. A higher truth emerges for me to embody: I AM completely and eternally innocent, healthy, connected, and free.

When I believe this, I am absolutely at peace. If I stray for an instant, I immediately find myself flirting with fear and delusion. This is true for you, too, and for everyone on Earth. When we find the truth, we know it to be the opposite of what we had previously thought was true.

My life with my mother taught me about the suffering that human beings endure. She also showed me that suffering takes many forms. Her suffering took the guise of a mental illness; growing up as her daughter formed mine. The other members of my family sculpted their versions as well, as does everyone in our greater human family. In the end, if we want to find compassion and peace, not only does "my" suffering, and "yours," and "my mother's" need healing, but our collective pain and fear must be released.

This compassion offers me deep serenity and intuitive guidance. I realize that God has no gender, but sometimes it helps me to imagine my Creator as a gracious and loving mother or father. In my human frailty, reaching out to Divine Parents keeps me on track. It provides me with an inner sense of safety and nurturance I rarely experienced as a child.

I am grateful for and humbled by the sacred power and perfection of my life, no matter what happened, and no matter what will happen.

Finding Peace

One day, I found a beautiful box on a shelf, high up in the back of my closet. In it, I'd placed some old treasures that meant a lot to me, although I'd forgotten a few. To my surprise, inside the box I found a message from my mother in the form of a Hebrew prayer she'd handwritten for me shortly before her death.

Carefully scripted in Hebrew and in English, it read:

May the Lord bless thee and keep thee;
May the Lord make His face to shine upon thee,
And be gracious unto thee;
May the Lord lift up His countenance upon thee,
And give thee peace.
—NUMBERS 6: 24–26

"Thanks, Mom," I thought, gazing at the page. "Go with God, and peace be with you, too."

Back to You and Your Process: Start with Forgiveness Lists

Just as I began my forgiveness journey by walking through the pain of my story with my mother, you will need to take an inventory of your victim-offender stories as well. When we have emotional attachments to pain, the stories seem very real to us. I honor that, but there's quite a bit more to it. In the end, they're all stories, containing valuable information hidden within them, and that's how we'll treat them in this book.

Many of the historical instances that stick most stubbornly in our minds are the ones with big teachable moments. They contain our soul themes, which need a dramatic moment (or series of moments) to get our attention.

Ask yourself, who or what remains unforgiven? If you knew you were going to die an hour from now, what situations would be revealed as obviously unresolved in your life? How about *subtly* unresolved? Include everything you can think of that doesn't feel peaceful inside you.

They Owe Me an Apology

First, make a list of every person, group, agency, organization, or company you would really like an apology from. Notice when your mind starts trying to edit the list by trying to convince you, "Oh, I've already worked on that" or "That wasn't really such a big deal." Just check in with yourself and be honest—do you want an apology or not? If your answer is yes, even a little bit, then write the person's or entity's name down. Look for subtle (and not so subtle) rivalries, jealousies, betrayals, and feelings of abandonment. Look under the rug—yes, investigate!

It may help to begin with today and then move back in time. Review your adult life, your teen years, your childhood, scanning your memories and the feelings within them for possible additions to the list. You may find a teenage crush; a failed marriage; unresolved business issues; a schoolyard bully; conflicts with siblings, teachers, friends, and, of course, your parents. Some people will pop into your mind instantly—they are the glaringly "guilty" culprits who still live with their stories inside you. Once you've written down the first layer of names, wait a while for more to come up. The subtler grievances you're holding on to will begin to emerge. Look for anger at God or the universe—you'll probably find that one, too.

As for what to include in the list, the more the merrier! The more people and situations and grievances you have on your list, the more signposts and landmarks you give yourself on your personal forgiveness map.

I Owe Him/Her/Them
an Apology

Once you've completed your first list, make a second one, with all the people, companies, groups, and so on that you feel *you* owe an apology. Again, if you're about to meet your maker in an hour (and you never know, so do the work now), with whom do you need to make things right? Think back to every situation in your life that you can remember.

Some people have a long list; some don't. It doesn't matter—you can always add to your list as you go deeper into the layers of your subconscious mind, where all this painful material is stored. When I made my forgiveness lists, I had plenty of people on them. I included my parents, former lovers, the two fathers of my children, a girl who bullied me in sixth grade (oh yeah, *she* definitely made the list!), the first boy who ever kissed me, and a few others. Anyone I had judged and made wrong at any time could qualify for either list—the first one because I had seen them as having wronged me, and the second because I had judged and belittled them, disregarding their true nature and my own. You can also add yourself to either or both lists, since self-forgiveness works in exactly the same way as forgiving someone else.

Readers familiar with twelve-step programs such as Alcoholics Anonymous, Narcotics Anonymous, and

Al-Anon will recognize that forgiveness lists bear a resemblance to step 4—"made a searching and fearless inventory of ourselves." For many people, step 4 is the most difficult part of the entire twelve-step process, because it involves so much humility, honesty, openness, and willingness. The lists are different because, in our forgiveness work, we aren't looking for our own "defects of character" as we would in twelve-step work. Yet making both kinds of lists compels us into a powerful process of removing our blankets of denial.

If you sincerely embrace and use these forgiveness lists, you will soon notice the healing, nourishing effect they have on your spiritual life. This is because the honesty needed to make the lists, and the sincere desire to heal the pain associated with each entry, leads you to readiness to experience the healing love of the One.

For help making forgiveness lists, you can go to www.anaholub.com to access free forgiveness list outlines that you can fill in and meditate on. Or, you can simply write your lists on a pad of paper. Handwriting your lists works best because it helps you connect to your emotions.

Further Thoughts on Apology

Even though you just went through the exercise of making your forgiveness lists by contemplating "Who owes me an apology?" and "To whom do I owe an apology?," I want to pause here to explore this further. Since apology and forgiveness are so linked in our minds, it's helpful to examine them both and see where they fit (or don't fit) in the flowing river of your forgiveness process.

A few years ago, I had the wonderful blessing of traveling to South Africa. I wanted to know how the truth and reconciliation process was coming along, some twelve years after the end of apartheid. In Cape Town, in Johannesburg, and along the southern coast, I interviewed many people from diverse backgrounds. I spoke with Xhosas, Zulus, Anglo South Africans, Afrikaaners, Muslims of Malaysian descent, South African Jews, and South Africans of mixed descent. Their answers to my questions were sometimes surprising and always fascinating.

One of the people I met had been active for decades in the struggle for equality and freedom, working tirelessly for South Africa on Nelson Mandela's team. He was a deeply committed, intelligent person, and he assured me that he would be ready to forgive once he received an apology from his former persecutors. He was waiting, very sure that remorse from the other parties was required before he could forgive. In his heart and mind, he was not open to beginning the forgiveness process until this occurred.

Even when I pressed him during the interview, this man was clear about his position. He told me he was right on the edge of forgiveness, ready at any moment, but was still waiting for the day when an apology would come. There was something inside him that told him to stop his inner process at this point, to refuse to go further until "the other side" made a conciliatory move.

Waiting for an apology can be a problematic healing strategy. Here are some of the pitfalls. Maybe you'll think of more.

1. **We give our power away.** If we wait for an apology, we may find ourselves waiting a long time. Indeed, we may *never* get an apology from the person who "wronged" us, and in the meantime, we put ourselves in the vulnerable position of waiting until someone else acts. This is a clear-cut example of giving our power away.

2. **The apology isn't good enough.** Even if we do get that apology, we may not like it. You've probably experienced this at some point in your life. The person apologized, but you judged it as "not good enough," for certain reasons that may even be unconscious to you. Perhaps you judged its length, its completeness, or—usually the case— the sincerity with which it was given.

3. **Apology seems impossible.** Perhaps the person is already dead or beyond the reach of any form of communication, and the option of receiving an apology from them seems impossible.

4. There's a standoff. Maybe the other person doesn't feel you have an apology coming and is, in fact, waiting for *you* to apologize! A standoff like this may never be resolved.

Apologies are important in the world of humanity, where we live together as if we were separate people. Separation is an illusion, but it's a powerful one, surviving because the collective "world mind" believes in it. As more and more of us relax into our foundation in Spirit, the illusion loses its strength. Still, apology can be very helpful in paving the way for reconciliation and healing on a world-of-humanity level. I honor the power of apology, while I'm careful to place it in its proper place as a tool for reconciliation between egos, not between souls.

Apologizing to God

I've described apology as a tool to expose the egoistic mind and to promote reconciliation in the world. But what about our need to apologize to our Creator for all the screw-ups we've made in our lives?

There's a fine line between apologizing to God out of guilt (and thus reinforcing guilt in our minds) and coming to Spirit in deep humility and readiness to release. Recognition that we strayed from the path, that we missed the mark and made errors of judgment, is essential—but what about our emotional/energetic frequency just *after* that recognition? Do we attack ourselves as poor, miserable sinners? Or do we have compassion for ourselves and treat ourselves as we would a loved one or a child who has erred? The choice is ours.

In the moment directly after an honest review of the facts, we decide whether to overlay our situation with guilt and shame or with compassion and humility. Western, industrialized culture (and other cultures, too) strives to keep us addicted to a downtrodden personal identity, sapping our life force and keeping us compliant and ignorant. This personal identity says to us, "See how I've screwed up? I'm just no good! The world is basically bad, and people can't be trusted. I need to hide my light under a bushel." If we come to the Great Mystery with this identity intact, we'll automatically recycle our pain rather than release it. This keeps us in bondage, individually and collectively, and perpetuates the status quo on Earth. It's bad for our health, and we can change it.

Change comes from making a different choice. To choose in a radically forgiving way, we must reroute the neural nets in our brains and merge with the wisdom of our one heart. Recognizing both our error and our intense desire for peace, we may come to Spirit in sorrow, yet with hope as well. If we trust deeply during the process, we will enter the river of love. If not, we'll interpret our prayers (and ourselves) as failures, and the cycle of sorrow will repeat itself again.

Ho'oponopono

The Hawaiian mystical philosophy of Ho'oponopono shows us the proper use of apology in a spiritual context. Based in ancient Hawaiian wisdom, it uses four statements to continually cleanse and heal our collective mind. The practitioner does Ho'oponopono on behalf of herself and all creation, seeing and understanding the interconnectedness of all life. These are the statements, in all their wonderful simplicity:

- I'm sorry.
- Please forgive me.
- I love you.
- Thank you.

By taking complete responsibility for everything that is happening—in the practitioner's life situation *and* the wider world—the practitioner apologizes to, asks forgiveness of, loves, and thanks not only another person but also the whole of all that is.

In the words of Dr. Ihaleakala Hew Len, a leading teacher of Ho'oponopono,

Ho'oponopono helps restore balance in the individual first, and then in all of creation ... All problems begin as thought. But having a thought is not the problem ... the problem is that all our thoughts are imbued with painful memories of persons, places or things ...

When you do Ho'oponopono, the Divinity takes the painful thought and neutralizes or purifies it. You don't purify the person, place or thing. You neutralize the energy you associate with that person, place or thing ...

Now something wonderful happens. Not only does that energy get neutralized; it also gets released, so there's a brand-new slate. The final step is that you allow the Divinity to come in and fill the void with light ..."[12]

There is something very powerful about entering sacred space with the intention to heal. During this healing, we may approach our Creator with thoughts of apology and remorse, stemming from images of ourselves as perpetrator, victim, or both. If this happens during your journey, remember that you want to *keep* the humble willingness you feel, and *release* any guilt or shame that comes up. If you take total responsibility for yourself and your intimate connection with all reality, you will invite deep inner cleansing, stillness, and light. This is the only healing there is.

---

12. Joe Vitale and Dr. Ihaleakala Hew Len, *Zero Limits: The Secret Hawaiian System for Wealth, Health, Peace, and More* (Hoboken, NJ: John Wiley and Sons, 2007), 45.

Readers who are experienced in working the twelve steps will notice obvious parallels here. Similar teachings are found in *A Course in Miracles,* Radical Forgiveness, and Ho'oponopono. Each practice uses different language, but the eternal truth of offering our burdens to the healing light of Spirit remains intact and pervades them all.

In conclusion, we remember that forgiveness does not depend on receiving or giving an apology to another person. Apology sweetens human interactions and provides glue for reconciliation in the world of humanity. As you explored earlier in making your forgiveness lists, apology is also a great tool for finding out where forgiveness has not yet occurred. These inner places became immediately obvious when you asked the question "Who owes me an apology?" To answer this question, your egoistic mind sprang into action with all the fear, anger, indignation, hurt, and feelings of betrayal that you had, consciously or unconsciously, within you. Now, aside from using our desire for it as a tool for forgiveness, we can let the idea of apology rest for now.

Telling Your Story

In your mind, there is a dramatic image, or picturing— perhaps several of them—of each person on your forgiveness lists. With each of these people or groups in your life, events happened, during which you perceived that a crime occurred. In the world of humanity, what happened may be a violent crime or it may be just a small blow to your ego. Either way, to you, something wrong occurred, and that is how your lists formed inside your mind.

Corresponding emotions link to each memory you hold. In this forgiveness process, you will delve into these memories and the emotions you hold about them. The purpose of this is not to wallow in the emotion, but to educate yourself about what already exists in your psyche. Examine what you have made there, and accept responsibility for the feelings that go with it.

Choosing an Item from Your List

For now, choose one item on your first forgiveness list. We will go through specific steps with this unforgiven part of your past (and present). When you're done, you can go back and visit every person, group, organization, idea, and so on, on each list, using the same steps. If you do this, you will be systematically clearing your "inner planes," or psychological and psychic landscape, of constricted places. By tracing the map of your consciousness (your forgiveness lists) with the healing power of the One, you will softly strengthen inside, in the most beautiful, holiest way possible.

Remember, the details of your story are important only as conduits of emotion. By telling your story, you want to access obvious and hidden emotions simultaneously, to the best of your ability. Once you really feel a lot of emotion, you've touched the constriction. At this point, more detail is not usually useful, so you can relax the part of your mind that wants to embellish or add to the drama.

> REMINDER: *No matter what details you have in your story, no matter how compelling they are to your mind, no matter how much blame you could conjure up toward yourself or another or others, take responsibility for what you're feeling. This emotional state is what you are bringing into this moment from the past. Take a moment to remember that the action is in the past and gone, even if it occurred a day, an hour, or a minute ago.*

H.O.W.

At this point, you may be asking, "How am I ever going to get to the deepest places of pain? I always feel numb or want to escape before I get there." To answer this question, I use H.O.W.: honesty, openness, and willingness.

We need honesty—direct, uncompromising honesty—to reveal to ourselves the beliefs we are carrying from the past. We also need lots of truth-telling to distinguish what is real from what we *thought* was true but is actually false (more on this later). We must be absolutely honest with the places inside our mind that we've hidden with denial up to this point; otherwise, no further healing can occur.

To this honesty, we add openness and willingness—the experience of revealing to Spirit our darkest thoughts, with trust that we will not be attacked or die in the process. We open to trust in divine love as the ultimate savior of our troubled little human self, not necessarily with any religious dogma—though you can bring it if you feel more comfortable—but with sincerity and a deep desire for inner peace. We lean on God/Goddess in much the same way that a twelve-step member leans on his or her Higher Power. *We admit that in the world of humanity there is no place else to go for healing, and we begin our journey with H.O.W. into the world of divine truth.*

With H.O.W., we stretch into

- **H**onesty with God,
- **O**penness to God, and
- **W**illingness to directly experience the grace of God.

Prayer and love are learned at the moment when prayer is impossible and your heart has turned to stone.
—THOMAS MERTON

An Example of H.O.W.

Here's a story from my life that illustrates H.O.W. I was traveling with my son, Aron, who was eleven years old at the time. We were in between flights at the Denver airport, having some pizza, and all seemed well. But when we arrived at the gate, we discovered, to my chagrin, that we had just missed our connecting flight! In a flash, I realized that I'd forgotten to advance my watch an hour to Denver time. I felt my face go red as I turned to apologize to my young son. *Oh, God,* I thought, *I'm such an idiot!*

Our situation was particularly horrendous in my mind because it was 8:00 p.m. and there were no other flights out of Denver to New York City that night. I knew this was an opportunity to forgive myself and the situation, to ask Aron's forgiveness, and to open myself with willingness to the perfection of the situation. Oy! I still felt like a total fool. Aron was very understanding and calm. He was giving me the compassion that I'd modeled for him so many times. At least *that* was a silver lining. With a big sigh, we got into the customer service line, with about forty people ahead of us.

Slowly we inched along the line. New dramas began to percolate in my mind, even though my soul was working hard to be in charge. "Remember," I told myself, "have vigilance only for God and His Kingdom."[13]

---

13. This is one of the lessons of the Holy Spirit given in *A Course in Miracles*, chapter 6.

All the same, I realized that if I had to buy new plane tickets on the spot, it could easily cost two thousand dollars or more. Wow, expensive mistake. Also, I'd have to pay for a hotel and a cab in Denver or else spend an uncomfortable, sleepless night in the airport, dragging my innocent son along for the ride.

"Okay, Beloved One, show me how this is perfect," I prayed as we finally got to the customer service counter. At this point, I completely surrendered to divine will, bringing my sheepishness with me and exhaling it into the universal compassion that I knew just had to be somewhere close by. The employees were finishing up a conversation about the guy ahead of me in line, who apparently had been acting like an arrogant, self-righteous jerk.

I explained to the woman behind the counter that we'd missed our flight, and she began checking the reservation. She looked up, puzzled. "Your incoming flight wasn't late," she said, "and the outbound flight went out on time. What happened?"

It was time for honesty. "I'm just having one of those days," I confided. "I forgot to set my watch ahead, and it was my fault we missed the flight. I really messed up. When's the next flight out?"

This woman was so kind, it brought tears to my eyes, which I showed her rather than hiding them. She began typing away, trying to get us out of Denver. I breathed and *opened* myself to more *honesty* and *willingness*. After a minute or two, she printed out a new itinerary. "How much is this mistake going to cost me?" I wondered.

The agent showed me the reservations for the next morning. Mustering up all my courage, I said, "How much are the new tickets?"

"Oh, I took care of that, dear. We can do that sometimes, for special cases. No extra charge." Wow, a miracle! But that wasn't all. "You'll need a hotel tonight, won't you?" she asked. "Here's a voucher for a room at half price. A free shuttle bus will pick you up as soon as you've made your reservation."

I was so grateful, I just about sat down right there and cried with joy. Instead, I took that sweet woman's hand and looked in her eyes. "You've been my angel tonight," I said. "Thank you so much! I will pray all good things for you."

She just smiled. "Thank you, dear," she said. "Next!"

As Aron and I walked toward our shuttle bus, I marveled at the lessons I had just learned. If I hadn't used H.O.W. in that situation and had been fearful instead, the customer service agent might not have channeled so much love back to me. Remember, the previous passenger had hassled her, so my inner state could have either added to her stress or relieved it. (As a soul, she is fully responsible for choosing her own actions, but she's also living in the world of humanity, just like me and just like the "jerk" before me.)

I felt intuitively that my mistake was perfect—it gave me a chance to practice H.O.W. and see the effects of my inner choices on my outer world. If I had chosen fear and hostility, who knows how much those new plane tickets, cab, and hotel would have cost? I didn't really want to find out. I just gave Spirit some gratitude instead.

Another result in this story was the effect of my energy on the crowd around me, on Aron, and on my body's physical systems. Leaning toward self-forgiveness and the possibility that my world was functioning in the perfection of the present moment, I focused on love through all levels of my being. If I had chosen differently, taking the familiar highway of fear and self-hatred, I would have exuded negativity into my bloodstream, toward my child (thereby teaching him that fear is an intelligent response to the world), and into the space around me. We make choices like this all the time, but we don't always notice their impacts. Energetically, we are intimately linked to one Creator. This means that our choice of fear or love infiltrates every cell of our physicality, as well as our relationships with family and friends, and oozes out to meet everyone and everything that crosses our path.

"Teach peace to learn it" is another axiom of wisdom from *A Course in Miracles*. We're all teaching each other about our choices all the time. We are naked to each other, pretending to be clothed. When we choose honesty, openness, and willingness as our teaching, the whole world comes deeper into peace.

Chapter Five

Step Three— Navigating the Emotional Body

Let's review the steps toward forgiveness you've taken so far: You imbued your space and time with prayer, making it sacred and asking for help from your Creator. Then you examined what is bothering you; i.e., what seems to be separating you from an experience of inner peace. This came in the form of the story you had in your mind about a "crime scene" that unfolded between you and another person(s), or you and yourself, or you and God. In the crime scene, you identified a victim and a perpetrator. You chose H.O.W. to examine your story about what happened. Now what?

Two Essential Ingredients

You'll notice that emotions are coming up to the surface. *To swim in the river of love, you must be willing to feel your feelings.* They will probably be uncomfortable and distressing—that's the nature of doing this sort of emotional clearing work. After all, if you felt great, you wouldn't need a book or a process to help you through it; you'd just go right ahead feeling great. But you're examining what doesn't feel great at all, and you'll need all the help you can get. At this stage and throughout your session, you'll need two essential ingredients: breath and more trust.

> *REMINDER: Remain consciously connected to the power of your prayers, and remember that you asked for help from the teachers and masters you invited into your sacred space. Come back to this support at any time during your process. These beings are here to help! Say YES to their wisdom and guidance.*

Breath

Focus on breathing, sending your breath throughout your body. You want its good oxygen and cleansing power right now. When emotional times get tough, we often hold our breath, and you'll want to be very aware of this tendency.

Gently remind yourself to breathe all the way into your belly. Bring breath into your head, throat, heart and lungs, diaphragm, belly, and all the way down to your toes and into the earth. Feel into your "back body" as well, bringing your inhalations and exhalations consciously to the place *behind* your heart and into your lower back. Breathe in and out of your heart. Feel the breath releasing out the bottoms of your feet and through your hands.

Breathing this way opens up your mind as well as your physical body. It gives your emotions room to travel, first into your full awareness and later out of your body and out of your mind.

Trust

Begin feeling whatever is coming up for you. Trust, then trust more. Keep it up!

Finding the Emotional Knot

Earlier I described emotional pain as a constriction, or knot, that lives inside our emotional bodies. *In this work, we want to learn from everything that is happening, so we don't push pain away or try to run from it. Instead, we gently lean into it.* When we relax into the process with an attitude of fascination, we're much more likely to get to the root causes of our sadness and trauma.

The deepest cause of pain is always the appearance that we've separated ourselves from the Great Mystery that gives us life. I say "appearance" because separation from Oneness is impossible. But when we believe separation is real, we give full power to the ego. We begin to feel alone, cut off from support, and vulnerable to attack. The ego's strategy is to retreat or defend, trying to protect our individuality against attack from the "outside" (as if there actually is an outside). We become afraid—petrified, in fact—because, after all, who's going to win a battle between you (or me) and God? Silly question—God wins every time. Therefore, we are terrified and want to hide.

For readers who have done a lot of psychotherapy, it might make sense to substitute "parents" for "God" in this scenario. After all, we were all small, vulnerable babies once. And parents are rarely perfect, so certain dysfunctional patterns of behavior often take root early in our development. But ultimately, the whole dance we do with our parents—or *any* authority figure—is just symbolic of our communion with, or fear of, our Source. Every conversation and interaction in our entire lives, even in the womb, is part of our constant conversation with our Creator. And when we feel dazed, shamed, and trapped by our ego—while we allow the ego to mess with us by making the fear seem real—we find ourselves on a battlefield. Although it looks like "me against the world," "me against the forces of evil," "me against my lover/boss/kid/ex," or "me against myself," it's really about me (and you) and how we feel about our relationship with our Source.

With our decisive jump into the river of love, we walk off the battlefield. We make a new commitment to peace. Swimming with determination and trust, we come out of hiding and face our fears. They are buried inside the constrictions we feel. Now, layer by layer, we will examine and release them.

Dissociation

If you've endured especially harsh incidents of violence, abandonment, or abuse in your life, you may have developed a pattern of dissociation. This means that sometimes you leave your awareness—and sometimes your body—as a strategy to help you survive. You might feel as if you're floating above yourself, or that time goes by and you've forgotten what you were doing. It's hard for you to stay connected to your bodily sensations and "stick around" during deep explorations. While dissociation is a natural coping mechanism that helped you get through terrifying events, as time goes on it can become a habit that will interfere with your healing.

You will need to relearn and remember (re-member—i.e., coming once again into your body) your connection to presence and awareness. At this point in your forgiveness process, you may need some extra guidance to give you direction and gentle reminders that life, as it is now, is safe enough to hold you. A coach or experienced therapist may be a helpful ally. Especially if you've had a series of abusive experiences over time, you'll probably need additional support from a loving, wise, and helpful professional. Please give this to yourself as a commitment to your healing. If you trust and ask for it, help will come.

Describe and Witness the Knot

In chapter 4, you made a list of victim/perpetrator stories, and selected one to begin. Now, remember the details of your chosen story. Start feeling all the aspects of your fear, pain, and anger. Using lots of trust and breath, keep your story about the crime in the forefront of your mind. Begin examining the sensations in your body.

Close your eyes so that your focus goes inside rather than outside. *Feel* into your body. What places are lighting up, sticking out, becoming obvious? Usually there's a spot that is connected with the grievance you are holding in your mind. This is your mind-body connection. It's real, and it needs your attention.

Your physical body is a reservoir for your unfinished mental and emotional business; it also holds all of your talent, love, and joy. Every incomplete, painful thought has been parked (by you) somewhere inside muscle, bone, and blood, waiting until you are ready to heal. You've chosen this moment to unwind these knots. It's time to find them and learn from them.

Often, my clients will report activity in their solar plexus (stomach area), heart, head, or throat. These areas are the knotting "hot spots," and you'll probably find something in one of those areas, or another zone that's particularly sensitive. If more than one spot wants your attention, just go to the hottest one first. By "hottest," I mean whichever one is the most dramatic or insistent. Since we're working layer by layer, you'll soon visit the other places as well.

Begin describing what the knot looks like and feels like. If you have trouble or lose direction, just go back to the story that gave rise to your emotion. Remember, you are tracing your trajectory from pain to healing by going from (1) the painful memory to (2) the painful emotions triggered by the memory to (3) the reservoir of pain you've stashed in your physical body.

The Story as Symbol

Get into the story enough to reach your feelings. Once you've contacted the feeling body and you have a path to travel from your emotions into your spirit, you don't really need the story anymore. So take your focus off the details of what happened, and concentrate more on the immediate, visceral experience of what is occurring in your heart and mind.

After all, the story is just a symbol. Your egoistic mind might really react to this statement. "What?" you may say. "Just a symbol? But these things really happened! I really *am* a victim (or perpetrator)! Real people were hurt! This is really, truly awful!"

My response to that voice, the one that wants to keep the victim consciousness alive, is that yes, in the world of humanity, where we appear to be individual human beings, the events really happened. And they *were* awful. But in the spirit world, the world of divine truth, we are eternal and untouched by the *maha lila* (Sanskrit for the "great show," or "play of illusion") that seems to be going on here on Earth.

When we make the choice to jump into the river of love, we actively choose to move from the world of victim consciousness into the world of the divine. From this perspective, all the stories that ever happened to you or anyone else are symbolic of our state of awareness.

Either we were aware of our union with eternal, perfect love when the story occurred or we weren't. And if we weren't aware, then we have a new chance to become aware—*now*. We can thank Spirit for this constant opportunity, patiently waiting for us until we are ready to join consciously with it—anytime, anywhere, under any circumstances.

This is the meaning of mercy.

Think about it. Hold the wonder of this divine, merciful generosity in your heart. It is truly miraculous. Unconditional love is where all miracles come from.

Back to the Knot

Once you've found the hottest constricted spot, begin to examine it in a spirit of exploration and curiosity. Ask yourself, "What *is* this?" And breathe. To help you get details and information about the nature of what author Eckhart Tolle calls your "pain body," [14] use the following questions:

- Where is the knot in my body?
- What does it feel like and look like?
- What colors do I see, and what textures do I feel?
- What am I feeling emotionally when I tune in to the knot?
- Is there a vision or image that comes to me?
- Am I afraid to look at it or feel it?
- Is there a memory connected to it? What is it?
- Is there anyone else with me? Who is it?
- Inside that knot, how old am I?

---

14. Eckhart Tolle, *The Power of Now: A Guide to Spiritual Enlightenment* (Novato, CA: New World Library and Namaste Publishing, 2004), 36.

• How do I hold any people in my image, vision, or memory? As better than me? Worse? More powerful? Scary? Stupid or unworthy? Evil? Notice the ego's need to maintain a power imbalance with the other people in your story.

Describe the constriction and learn as much about it as you can. Listen to it for messages. See the colors and textures of it. Notice the feeling that's connected to the physical sensations and to the thoughts and beliefs in your mind. Call on courage and mercy. Witness and feel.

Describing the Knot

Use the following thoughts and guidelines to help you get details and information. Write your responses down if you want to, or just use the questions to support your process.

1. *Where* are the emotional knots that want my attention now? Examples: belly/gut/solar plexus, heart, throat, jaw, head, and so on.
2. The first knot I want to focus on is_____.
3. Describe the knot—its texture, color, visual image, movement, etc. Examples: hard, elastic, grainy, rough, splintered, gooey, black, red, tarry, rocky, and so on.

4. Breathe! Focus on a long, slow exhalation to relax even deeper.

5. Ask for help from the masters, angels, and teachers you have invited into your sacred circle.

6. TRUST. Use H.O.W. to know how to trust. Be honest, open, and willing to do this work.

7. Check this place out again. Describe any additional colors, textures, or images you receive.

8. If you'd like to use these questions in a printed form for easy reference, visit www.anaholub.com and download a free copy of "Describing the Knot" and "Questions for the Knot."

The Feeling Tone

Remember that the "feeling tone" of the constriction is its vibration. Just like a musical note sounded on a guitar string or a piano, the note struck by your constriction spot will sing. Listen to it and feel its vibratory rate. Hint: it will be low and dense, not high and joyful. Why? Because the feeling tone describes, without words or intellectual thoughts, the victim story's effect on your consciousness. It is a wound, and it shows you how it survives within you. You may not hear it with your ears, but you will recognize it nonetheless.

The crime scene you're focusing on is not isolated, but is connected to a string of *other times and places in your life when you've experienced the same feeling tone before*. It's a note, a sound, a vibration. Is it familiar? Be still and listen, allowing the memories to arise naturally from your subconscious mind.

Some memory, or perhaps a whole string of them, will probably come up. They were other healing opportunities that you didn't recognize at the time. You didn't have the maturity, readiness, or skills to deal with it then, but you do now. If nothing comes up, that's okay, too.

Some Examples of Knots

Over the course of doing healing work for the past twenty-five years, I've encountered many different descriptions of emotional knots. Some came from my own experience of the subconscious mind, and some came from my clients. Certain archetypal images often arise. These examples are offered to give you clues, but of course, you should go with your own direct experience. Trust what you receive, and go with it. There isn't a wrong way to do this!

Whatever comes to you is right for you. As you insist on examining the truth, you will travel deeper and deeper into the reservoirs of past pain that you've held in your body. The images will change as you continue to explore, and the knot's location in your body may shift along the way. Your body's wisdom will begin to work for you. Let it. Allow deep contact with this wisdom. It isn't hard; it just takes honesty, openness, and willingness. Your physical, emotional, and mental bodies will be cheering and celebrating your choice to delve in, because healing is on its way at last.

Something to remember at this point is that the constriction you find is actually energy. It's vibrational. So if, during this part of your exploration, you find images that are filled with light and angels, it's a good clue that you aren't doing the work. The crystallization of fearful thought—which is full of pain, shame, anger, and guilt—will look and feel that way: painful and guilty. The image will match the feeling tone of your memories. So don't do a "spiritual bypass." In other words, don't skip the hard parts so you can get all comfy with light and love. *This work, and the tough honesty it takes, is light and love in the form of truth.* A spiritual bypass won't help you; in fact, it'll just slow you down. Go straight for an honest description of the anguish that you feel. You'll find it growing out of your victim story.

Colors and textures often appear when we examine emotional knots. More than one client found a gray ball of slimy, snakelike creatures. Clients often find images of tangled serpents, intestines, or ropes, usually in dark colors. Sometimes the color brown comes up, mirroring self-disgust, or feeling "like a piece of shit." Many people encounter black, rigid boulders in their bellies, or caves of darkness in their hearts, or feelings of suffocation, or images of a desert. At times, the descriptions are full of red, fire, and anger.

Going into your body to find places of pain *is* the journey of going into your subconscious to find your shadow side. Many archetypal symbols are alive down there. You may find links to great epics and legends of diverse cultures. As Carl Jung and Joseph Campbell showed us, all cultures are actually alive and well inside the collective unconscious mind that we share. You are participating in your own hero's journey, going on a quest to find the treasure buried in your own mind. There will be tests and trials, but once you get a feel for the territory, what shows up there ceases to be intimidating and begins to be intriguing—if you let it.

Some people are much more visual than others. I'm not especially visual, though I'm very intuitive and kinesthetic. I feel my process deeply, but I don't necessarily get an image to go with it, or if I do, it may be quite simple. Some my clients are very visual—they regularly get lots of colorful information and images. The point here is, don't get hung up on the *way* that data comes to you, and don't try to push or pull it along. This is about relaxing and surrendering, not marching in to conquer something.

The psychological information is already living inside you, so let it speak. Tune in to the visual input you get and explore it, and also expand into what your other senses are telling you. You may feel hot or cold areas in your body, or smells, or little muscular tics or twitches that tell you to concentrate on a particular place. If you use H.O.W., you'll find the constriction, and if you need help, you can always get a coach or therapist to guide you.

It doesn't matter whether you've had lots of experience doing this kind of work or this is your first time ever. In fact, if you've been exploring New Age concepts, you may have to set many of them aside just to become "simple" enough inside yourself to do this work successfully. Put aside your tried-and-true methods of aligning your chakras, reading your energy, or assessing how astrology fits in with all this. You won't need any other skill set or knowledge now, and you can always come back to other methods later if you wish.

Here's an example of what I'm talking about. A client I'll call Nancy had her ego firmly ensconced in an identity of being a "healer." She was so sure she had already worked on her issues that she never really got close to the emotional release that is the cornerstone of this practice. In fact, she actually used her experience as a buffer, or shield, between herself and the new possibilities she could have during our session. Even though I did my best to guide her deeper, she kept saying, "Yeah, I did that years ago, and ..." or "I already know I have issues with my mother." Nancy clearly wanted help (she did make the appointment, after all), but she wasn't honest, open, and willing enough to do her own work, inside her own mind and body. Nothing I could say would change that.

By the time most people come to me, they're eager to move their energy. But Nancy was not. She is worth describing, in case you recognize yourself in her. In fact, we've all been in Nancy's shoes more times than we might like to think. Every time we've allowed our egos to rule instead of asking the Great Mystery to guide us, we've "pulled a Nancy"—maybe for lifetimes!

Nick was a very different sort of client. When he came to me, he was sixty-five and had been an emergency medic all his working life. Nick was a man of strong principles who had spent thirty years attending church. Because he didn't know how to release his painful emotions, he had chosen alcohol as a way to self-medicate, and by now his strategy was backfiring mightily. He had no knowledge of how to handle his anger and anguish, so he took his pain out on his wife. Between the alcoholism and the domestic abuse, things were really deteriorating for Nick, but he came with an eager readiness to learn H.O.W. to turn his life around.

Nick had never been to a self-help session in his life. He didn't believe in AA, and he'd had too much pride to seek help earlier. Being a medic, similar to being a soldier or a cop, his professional culture didn't support admitting that he had a problem—he just swallowed his emotions and kept going. But now everything was falling apart, and Nick was terrified that his wife would finally leave him. Nick had finally hit bottom: he was humbled to the point of real openness to anything that would truly help him. Nick was in the perfect place to sincerely explore his inner landscape.

It turned out that although Nick had never waded into these waters before, he was a natural swimmer in the river of love. He had never felt comfortable with the dogma of the church, but he had a direct connection with Spirit. This gave him a way to contact his interior life with faith and flexibility.

When we began our session, Nick trusted me completely. He was going by gut feeling, and his gut told him this work would lead him out of his misery, so he dove in wholeheartedly. As he explored his victim stories, he began feeling his emotions. And as he opened to feeling, he found an emotional knot in his heart. Following my instruction, he slowed down and courageously began examining and feeling, deeper and deeper.

Nick found that his heart was barricaded with old wooden boards. Since he grew up in a ranching family, this symbolic image came right out of his childhood. Nick tuned in to himself and asked many of the helpful questions: *In the scene or image, how old was I? Where was I? Was I alone or with someone else? Were there memories attached to this image in my heart?*

Nick let the answers to these questions come naturally. He was learning about himself. His experience was visceral as he felt the deep desire for protection that had prompted him to erect these barriers. He looked the "fear of fear" squarely in the eye. Then he took responsibility for both the construction and the deconstruction of the barricade around his heart, allowing the old wooden boards to come down—not knowing what would happen next. This was an act of sheer trust on Nick's part. His valiant effort was a result of the raw sincerity he had come to—all because his life no longer worked. He knew it was a choice he wanted and needed to make.

Nick was able to allow himself healing contact with Spirit, which was his own spiritual intelligence, only after he dismantled the barricades around his heart. He found new space within himself for intuitive wisdom to flow. As long as he stayed connected to Spirit (which took some practice over time), he had no desire for alcohol and treated his wife with respect. This is why we pray and release our pain *first,* before we go looking for answers to life's big questions. Like Nick, we need to listen with honesty and make room for a new vibration within us.

Chapter Six

Step Four—
Embracing Fear
with Love

Over the years, while being a student of life on my own path and a professional forgiveness counselor to many, I've discovered that what our spiritual awakening looks like on the outside doesn't really matter: our shifts of consciousness may be flamboyant or extremely subtle, and most likely they will fall somewhere in between. Except in a few rare cases, awakening happens within us in thousands of tiny baby steps. Some are obvious and life-changing, but many are often mysterious and not even available to our conscious mind. As we grow in our process, the shifts become more and more conscious, but even then there are vast levels of our being that, for most of us, are hidden throughout our entire human lifetime.

The softness I've grown into during the past twenty-five years is due to the influence of my love for the Divine Mother. This aspect of the One provides us with gentle strength, being impervious to the egoic mind. She has no need to prove and no dramatic, sassy performance. Her love is universal and tender; it gently supports us, sometimes so subtly that if we aren't in touch with wonder and awe at the little miracles of our day, we miss it entirely. But that's okay, because this blessing is always here, waiting for us to remember it again and again, becoming brighter with each knot of pain we release from our hearts and minds.

I mention this soft power here because, as you go to the edges of whatever constriction you've discovered, you may be amazed by your response to it. You may have a big burst of emotion and revelation, or you may just breathe out and feel lighter. What it looks or feels like doesn't matter. Over time, you will experience a myriad of variations on the theme. What matters is the *direction* of healing you choose, and the sincere prayer you use to guide you.

Just as many Muslims face Mecca five times each day, we face our original innocence again and again. With sincerity, we disrobe before our Creator. Which veils drop to the ground, and whether they are of heavy burlap or fine silk, is unimportant. *Just stay focused on the unveiling.* For after all, at this stage in our evolution, we're an entire planetary species of strip-tease artists. Take it all off, then take it off again!

Approaching the Edges of the Knot

Once you've found the tightness in your body and described it to yourself with honesty, openness, and willingness, you have three options:

1. You can choose to retreat from the pain.
2. You can decide to battle the pain.
3. You can lean gently toward the pain.

Let's explore each of these options.

Option 1: Retreating from the Pain

This method is humanity's most familiar mode of operation. We've all done it a million times, over countless lifetimes.

If you retreat from the pain, it means that at this point in your exploration, because of the mental, emotional, and psychic discomfort that is arising, you stuff your suffering (and its wisdom) back down into the reservoir of your body. Here it continues to fester, attracting additional circumstances into your life as new opportunities to heal. "Not now, God," you say. "I don't want to deal with this, my own custom-built creation of misery. I just want this pain to go away. Leave me alone. I'll handle it another day." Since we are, in truth, eternal, and we have also been given free will, we can make this choice as often as we like. And most of us make it daily, hourly, and minute by minute—and don't even realize it!

Denying our pain explains society's dependence on painkillers and antidepressants. Instead of choosing to allow divine healing, we self-medicate. It's worth examining your lifestyle choices to get a sense of how much "stuffing" of sadness, fear, and pain you're doing to yourself. If you're indulging in any addictive or avoidant behaviors (including drug and alcohol abuse, workaholism, excessive TV watching/video game playing, unhealthy eating habits, excessive worrying, and craving attention and approval, to name a few), you have a map of your ongoing retreat from freedom and release. These behaviors are all feeble attempts at filling a gaping cavern of loneliness and separation from Spirit. They never work, and not only that, our experience of separation is a false one. But we'll never know the truth unless we demand more courage of ourselves. Retreat will only get more and more painful and sickening (literally) over time.

Option 2: Battling the Pain

You want help, but you choose the old paradigm to try to get it. Being psychically steeped in war and violence, you *attack* the fear by staging a showy assault. The outcome must produce a winner and a loser. You speed up your thinking and try an "Out, damned spot! Out, I say!" strategy.[15] In a display of individual power, you pull out the big guns—that is, all your coolest techniques—and do your best to vanquish your fear through brute force. This might include zapping the knot, exercising like a maniac, fasting for days, calling on spiritual beings with swords to cut the pain out of you, or burying your suffering in the ground.

The techniques involved aren't important; it's the attitude you employ them with that makes the difference. Everything about this inner healing work is *energetic,* so examine your emotional stance in relation to your own pain. Do you really want to get rid of it? If so, you'll do everything in your power (using your personal power, which is an illusion and, therefore, won't ever work) to eliminate suffering from your body. You will assume that it's your body that needs to change, and you will fixate on being "strong," in the old-school sense of the word. The thing is, there's no learning going on here, just a deep addiction to comfort and maintaining the status quo. If you *fight* your pain, you're still on the battlefield. Nothing has

---

15. Shakespeare, *Macbeth,* Act V, Scene 1.

changed, and as long as you're fighting, you won't be able to invite the healing power of forgiveness to heal you.

Option 3: Leaning Gently Toward the Pain

When you lean in gently toward the pain, the pulse of your healing comes into coherence with the vitality of life. With calm determination and an attitude of experimentation, you continue to ask your spiritual partners for help. You add a remembrance of the divine feminine energy (no matter whether you're physically male or female). You breathe, slow down some more, and listen with patience. You invoke compassion as your saving grace and let your body teach you about unwinding and releasing. This method is what surrendering into divine love is all about.

> *A wise teacher teaches through approach,*
> *not avoidance.*
>
> —*A COURSE IN MIRACLES*,
> CHAPTER 6: TO HAVE, GIVE ALL TO ALL

Your Choice

If you choose option 3, you are ready to lean gently toward your pain. This choice takes more breath, more trust, and more sincerity than the other two, and I am with you right now thanking you for your courage.

Very few of us have had much previous training in leaning gently into discomfort of any kind. In modern Western culture, many of the epic stories we learned as children taught us either to win in battle, to be manipulative to get what we want, or to run away and hide. Watching our parents and other adults, we probably got some of those messages at home as well. When we lean in with gentleness, we choose the path of divine feminine wisdom instead. We trade our battlefield for a classroom where we focus on learning instead of warfare. Leaning in, we pioneer a new way of living.

Looking in the Mirror

If we really want to know the truth about ourselves and our relationships, we have to get past seeing everyone else as the reason our world doesn't work. While it's true that some people do some pretty ugly stuff, it's not true that you and I have nothing to do with it. Each crime story on your first forgiveness list about you (as victim) and another (as offender) contains some kernel of truth about you.

I learned this lesson in a graphic way one day while contemplating my disgust and anger over the U.S. government's involvement in the Iraq war. It was during the early days of the invasion by the United States into Iraq, ostensibly to rout out weapons of mass destruction. The president and his administration were not fully truthful with the American people, initiated war for dubious reasons, and killed and maimed hundreds of thousands of Iraqi and U.S. citizens. As a peace activist, I was overcome with horror at the carnage.

I was in a workshop with Colin Tipping, one of my forgiveness mentors, at the time. "What's the hardest part for you about the war?" he asked us. For me, it was the wanton greed of the decision makers. I felt they started the war to keep the war machine and its profits surging and to ensure access to oil pipelines in the Middle East. People were being murdered and land laid to waste by this greed. I just couldn't stand it.

In the forgiveness exercise that followed, we examined our victim stories. Mine was easy. Plenty of curse words could describe it. "Those @#$%ers are greedy! They're killing innocent people!" The second part was not so simple, however, because we then had to find the same qualities within ourselves. "Me, greedy?" I said to myself. "I'm not greedy. I go out of my way to be generous with my money and my time. In fact, I work hard to make sure I'm *not* greedy."

Going deeper, I found the inner contraction of all my anger and blame. The top layers focused on the obvious—my government leaders and their wrongdoing. When I turned it around to look at myself, I noticed how being greedy was a quality I actively didn't want to consider as part of my identity. Other people were greedy, not me!

I needed to delve even deeper into my psyche. I found a fear there, projected outward to "others," that maybe, in fact, I was greedy, and didn't like myself because of it. With my breath and sincerity, I kept looking until I could find greed in me. I'm human, after all, and that means that all human qualities can be found in me as well as everyone else.

Even though I am often a generous person, I saw that there were times when I'd been greedy for security, for attention, and for love. Maybe it wasn't money I wanted, but greed can affect life in many forms. I remembered times when I had been greedy for credit for my accomplishments, especially at school. As a child, I was greedy for compliments in another competitive field, ballet, where what I looked like before the mirror and on stage was prized beyond the joy of artistic expression. This was a humbling realization. I'd never discovered this place within me before, and even though my ego recoiled from it, I also knew it was true. My soul loved the whole exploration, because it was leading me to a great realization.

Once I found the greed inside as well as outside myself, I could lay *all* of it before Spirit for healing. My acceptance of this "ugly" quality within myself as well as in others was required for true peace. After radically forgiving the entire situation, I could feel compassion for everyone and anyone who ever felt greed constrict their heart. I saw how greed stems from fear, and it feeds on the anxiety that there will never be enough for everyone. I'd felt that plenty of times in my life, and I could bless those who felt it, too. This didn't mean that I now supported the war. Not at all! But my heart was freed from the self-righteous anger that sapped my life force. I still work for peace. At the same time, I honor the beauty that lies deep within every person... even those who wage war.

When we can see ourselves on both sides of the duality equation, and can offer all of it to Spirit, then we open the door to "the peace that passeth all understanding." We learn that we are neither victim nor perpetrator in our heart of hearts. In reality, we are free.

To deepen into the experience of leaning toward your suffering in order to heal it, remember that your victim/perpetrator story is a symbol for your awakening. It includes circumstances that life gave you, and *interpretations* of those circumstances that *you gave yourself*. It leads you to the soul themes that you are working on in this lifetime. The story of what happened is an arrow pointing to the knot of constriction. It's the knot that captures your attention now, and *the knot is really a temple of transformation*. So focus on the raw experience of the constriction itself. The details of the story will drop away at this point, because they're no longer needed. If you notice yourself drifting out of your forgiveness process, come back to the story to reconnect yourself with the fear, sadness, and guilt it represents. Remember, you want to go *toward* the pain gently, to learn from it and then release it.

The Tricky Part

We lean toward our suffering with deep compassion. Respecting the knot means we don't just go barreling into the middle of it, but softly touch its edges. Being engaged with the emotions that are coming up, we need to breathe fully, with lots of trust. As the fear, pain, anger, and sadness come forth, we exhale them to make room for more vitality and life force. This is a universal method of healing, and it works the same way for everyone.

To help you to stay present during the process, do the following:

- Be honest
- Go gently toward the knot with a willingness to heal
- Open your mind to receive the teachings
- Breathe deeply

Okay, ready for a little secret? This isn't the hard part. The difficult aspect of this work is shifting your focus *from* identifying with the suffering *to* the vast love that exists beyond suffering.

We've all spent decades (perhaps millennia) practicing attachment to personal pain, and we've gotten pretty damn good at it. The attachment is so familiar and so socially accepted that to expand beyond it demands our complete attention. The reassuring part about this is that no matter how mired we've become in a false, ego-driven identity, everyone has the capacity to link with the immense, expansive quality of life. Because our true self is Infinite Being, no one is left out in the cold.

At this point, we become aligned in consciousness with Spirit, which is far bigger than the small world of our pain. Expanding, we hold the pain in the palm of our hand, to examine it, learn from it, and bless it on its way out of our heart and mind.

It is a delicate dance to feel the intensity of the emotions as they arise, and to witness them with compassion. Knowing that we are linked to a greater whole (even if we have no idea what, who, or where it is) takes huge trust to start, and lots of inner strength to maintain.

The first time a big inner expansion happens within you, it can feel like dissociation. Even those of us who haven't experienced abuse may begin to space out right about here. The difference is that we maintain *contact* with the messages we're receiving, *awareness* of our body, and *consciousness* of our thoughts about the process. We become larger than the knot, but we don't go away. We refuse to become distracted by our usual thought patterns. Instead, we link to divine love in our knowledge and conviction that our Source is the only true healer. With humility, we embrace our memories, distrust, and betrayal of self and others with the kindness we would extend to a sick child or a friend in need.

Surrounding misery with our expanded consciousness, we also remember to ask for help from the angels, masters, and wise ones inside our sacred space. The wisdom of creating a sacred space in the beginning is dawning on us now, when we need the comfort and protection of its sanity in the midst of our insanity. The sacred space becomes both a place to reach out to for assistance, and an inner home to rest in while we stretch ourselves into new areas of consciousness. Our opening prayer comes back to us now, giving us sustenance, intention, and purpose.

We are crossing the bridge of forgiveness. Mercy comes to greet us, just as it embraced the prodigal son. This blessing is well beyond the capacity of our small human minds, but we enjoy it with reverence nonetheless. We feel the soft touch of the Divine Mother as we make our way across the bridge, beyond our mistaken thoughts of separation, leaning toward the One.

Chapter Seven

Step Five—
Listening for
Hidden Messages

Up to this point, you have reached the constriction of suffering within your body and have begun exploring it. You've described it to yourself and continually worked with breathing through any discomfort so that you remain present. You've asked for help from your team of spiritual advisers and drawn strength from the sacred space you created at the beginning of your session. Now it's time to listen deeply to your body and your mind as the knot frees up its hidden messages.

Reactions and Responses
to the Ego

Many of the world's sacred, cultural, and psychological traditions explore the phenomenon of the "split mind." This is our unified, holy mind, which is created by God, divided into two segments to make duality. As *A Course in Miracles (ACIM)* describes it, the split mind is an illusion, constructed by our belief that we have separated from the One. Since the separation never really happened, we are living in an insane world, where what seems real is not, and what is real appears hidden. *ACIM* goes further to explain that God's creation, stemming from perfect love, is eternal, desirable, abundant, and forever true. The text contrasts divine *creation* with what the ego *made*. It says the ego dreams an "unhappy dream." Into this dream we place all the fear, suffering, and delusion we experience when we buy into separation and its loneliness.

Since we made up our suffering, we are the only ones who can unmake it. Since, in truth, we are holy—and, therefore, absolutely responsible for ourselves—we must release and cleanse all falsehood by offering it to the only true source of life. This is the path to sanity, service, and heaven on earth.

> *A split mind cannot perceive its fullness, and*
> *needs the miracle of its wholeness to dawn upon*
> *it and heal it.*
>
> —*A COURSE IN MIRACLES*, CHAPTER 7:
> THE CONSISTENCY OF THE KINGDOM

Because an ego is standard operating equipment on this planet, we can assume that yours is alive and well. It's working full-time, constantly re-creating the illusion of a self-as-separate existence for you; that is, it's doing its job while being under the illusion that God is dangerous and untrustworthy—and, therefore, life itself is also dangerous and untrustworthy.

As we begin to recognize the characteristics of the ego, we begin telling ourselves stories about why it does what it does, and whether this is a "good" thing or a "bad" thing. We have several choices regarding how we perceive the ego and our basic attitudes toward it. Let's look at them here.

Choice 1: The Ego Is Bad; Therefore, We Must Get Rid of It

Because the ego is sometimes described as a "pain body," some people then make the leap toward eviscerating it. (This is not what Eckhart Tolle suggests, but people do it anyway.) They want to get rid of the ego so they can finally experience peace. Because it is the author of so much suffering, they think it deserves to die! While this is an understandable reaction, notice how it keeps us squarely on the battlefield. Going back to chapter 6, we can see that blaming the ego and making it "wrong" is choosing option 2: battling the pain. We go with the "Out, damned spot!" policy because we've assumed that yet another thing in life is BAD.

If you listen with this attitude to the messages that emerge from your physical, emotional, and mental pain, you will naturally try to spar with them. You'll want them to change, because you'll assume they are wrong from the start. You'll see a reflection of how you hold WHO YOU ARE to be wrong, bad, sinful, or evil to begin with. This is not the way to swim in the river of love—it's simply a familiar way to stand on the shore and *pretend* to swim. But we all know that pretending is not the same as actually jumping in and getting wet! Watch for habits of battling the ego. They may come up again and again.

Choice 2: The Ego Is Our Champion and Protector

Another popular way of describing the ego is as our champion and protector, a key ally on our spiritual path. How could we ever have gotten along without it? Don't we need to develop an ego just so that we can dismantle it later on? Or perhaps we need to keep vestiges of an ego around even as we open to our spiritual path—the old "trust in God but tie your camel first" approach. This stance suggests that it is actually glorious to be an individual, and we wouldn't want to miss out on *that*.

In this camp, the ego is appreciated as a guardian, acting in a Freudian sense as a superego who puts a lid on our id (the little monster who's gotten out of control). We just need to teach it manners and tell it to sit quietly in the corner, and all will be well.

While it's true that we need our mind and intellectual capacity to function here on Earth, it is not therefore true that our intellect needs to run the show. Once we've consciously chosen a direct link to forgiveness, our mind *serves* our true self, not the other way around. So watch to see if you are clinging to your ego to maintain your sense of mental prowess or some semblance of sanity. Ego is not where sanity resides, but it can seem that way—if you believe what the external world has been telling you since day one.

Choice 3: Observe What Is, without Evaluating

I encourage observation without evaluation when you're going deep into introspection. Notice how, the moment we begin categorizing the ego, we're in it ourselves. If we need to make the ego wrong, we battle it. And if we take offense at making it wrong and instead begin to champion it, we're still making a case for keeping separation, even if at a subtle level.

As the old Sanskrit expression reminds us, "Neti neti"—not this, not that. Not good, not bad. Just *is*. We have an ego until we don't. What can we learn from it?

Either there is an experience of oneness or there is not. Being on a spiritual path is all about which of these possibilities we choose, moment to moment. If we are focused on oneness above all, then we'll be able to discern the truth about the messages we receive from the knots we find within us. If not, we'll become confused or go back to our familiar, comfortable falsehoods, thereby recycling rather than releasing our pain.

Within the oneness are uncountable layers of creation, nesting inside each other in a fractal structure, like Russian dolls fashioned to fit one inside another. This is where we find levels of individuality—from separate people, families, and lifetimes to distinct languages, cultures, genders, times, and places. It all fits together without argument, without complaint. The appearance of individuality is another manifestation of the constant, infinitely creative artwork of the divine. It is the One arising as many, the Buddhist "ten thousand things." We can see ourselves as innumerable tendrils of conscious experience at play inside the matrix of Being.

The First Layer of Messages

As we deepen our honest exploration of suffering, we first encounter the messages of the ego. This represents the top-tier stuff of our mind; these messages live closest to the surface, which makes them easiest to find. What we do with them once we find them will depend on whether we've chosen to battle, champion, or simply *observe* the information we receive.

Cindy, one of my clients, is a case in point. Cindy had a horrific childhood. Her mother, father, stepfather, and neighbor all had dramatic parts to play in her life. The intersecting soul connections of her spiritual family gradually became clearer for her during the course of our work together. Here's her story.

Cindy was abused verbally, physically, and sexually as a child. All went relatively well until she was about six years old, when her mother divorced her father and remarried. The new husband was a lawyer and well respected in the community. What Cindy soon came to find out, though, was that her new stepfather was also a pedophile. He began abusing Cindy without mercy. Instead of protecting her, Cindy's mother grew jealous of the sexual attention her new husband was lavishing on her daughter. The entire family hid the terrible violence behind closed doors. Cindy retreated into her room and protected herself as well as she could.

One of the major strategies Cindy's ego devised was to be the "perfect girl": passive, meek, and quick to hide. She developed a habit of looking over her shoulder that lasted into adulthood. She buried her rage deep inside, where she could not consciously feel it, so that she could continue to survive. Fortunately, she had a talent for music, and so her guitar became a major ally. She spent long hours by herself in her room, strumming and dreaming.

Eventually, Cindy grew up, moved out of the house, and began life on her own. She dabbled in different forms of therapy, which helped put her in touch with some of the rage she felt. She confronted her mother about the abuse and cut off all ties with her stepfather.

When we began forgiveness counseling together, Cindy was in her mid-thirties, living in a small apartment with her cat. She was miserable. Because she had a repeating pattern of sabotaging all her relationships, including those with her bosses and coworkers, she couldn't keep a job. Things would start out well, then quickly sour. With every job and every romantic relationship, Cindy was continually reliving the patterns of her childhood.

As we gently explored together, Cindy began to touch the knots of despair and pain that had formed inside her. She felt them in her body, her emotions, and her mind. Courageously she stripped away layers of denial so that she could get down into the deeper levels of belief she had developed about herself and her world. She used H.O.W. to love herself just as she was, with honesty, openness, and willingness.

Not surprisingly, Cindy encountered many messages that she had buried for years. I want to point out—emphatically—that although I'm using Cindy as an example, I've also either personally gotten all the messages that Cindy received, or heard them emerge from other clients. *In other words, the ego messages we receive are universal and archetypal. They stem from the ego's constant drive to maintain a state of mind that separates, divides, compares, attacks, and defends.*

Externalized Thoughts

Since Cindy experienced so much trauma in her life, including abuse by her mother and stepfather and abandonment by her father, you might think that her internalized messages would be outwardly focused—that the messages would come out sounding like "I hate you!" and "You betrayed me!" Cindy's human personality was very familiar with these thoughts, but they were not hidden messages—they were the obvious thought patterns that she had given space to inside her mind, day in and day out. These thoughts focus on the other people in Cindy's life, blaming them with anger and resentment.

You, too, will be aware of your conscious thoughts about your victim and perpetrator stories. These externalized thoughts are tales of woe, which, when we believe them and make a whole life out of them, bring us constant pain and sorrow. If you haven't forgiven an ex-lover or ex-spouse for a painful breakup, if you still blame your parents for the way they raised you, if you feel cheated out of money or a career advancement, or even if you haven't yet examined and released the pain of a violent crime, you will have thoughts of recrimination and revenge (even if subtle) and feelings of anger, fear, and resentment. These thoughts and feelings are directed at the other people involved, and include the complex of your victim or perpetrator story. Nothing's hidden here—except, perhaps, the depth to which you are attached to the story as part of your identity.

Self-Pity Is Married to Blame

Notice how self-pity plays a part in holding any blame scenario in place. In fact, self-pity can be present any time you complain about life. It's easy to feel sorry for yourself, to host a big old "pity party." Whole days or weeks might vanish into a quagmire of depression or anger because of self-pity. You might have a habit of talking about your victimhood with friends, and maybe your friendships are based on a mutual blaming of others. Doing this releases a biochemical rush of cortisol and adrenaline in your bloodstream that can be dangerously addictive. It's a convenient way to hold on to habitual thoughts about your predicament, externalize them onto others, and never take a deep look in the mirror to see yourself.

Watching how you speak will give you lots of great information about your relationship with self-pity. Do you say things like, "I got sold up the river" (a slavery image), "I got bit in the butt" (a root chakra/survival fear image), "They threw me (or others) under the bus," or "I got stabbed in the back"? Listen to how you use language and you'll see some of your unconscious blame and self-pity. Then decide if you'd like to change what you say to reflect a higher consciousness.

Though I'm being very direct here, I'm not trying to disregard or diminish any pain you went through during a terrible time in your life. With compassion, I'm asking, "Do you want to keep it, or let it go?"

Deciding to Go Deeper

You may want to write in your journal about your externalized thoughts, but since you've already told yourself the story in step 2, they are probably already included in your process. What we're after here in step 5 are the hidden messages that you've linked to this story but weren't aware of before. You'll find them buried in your body, inside the constrictions of fear you found in step 3. By offering compassion, in step 4, you've given the blockage some space to begin softening. This softening opens the door to listening, discovering, and learning.

You'll find that the messages are more about how you feel about yourself—because of assumptions you've made about your life and life in general—than how you feel about other people. *This is why self-forgiveness is the deepest place we can go to heal.* Compassion transports us away from self-hatred, healing it

with the power of Spirit. But before we can wash ourselves clean with the holy water of this river, we must
be aware of our wounds, and we must confront the
full extent of their destructive force.

Revealing Hidden Messages

Finding the hidden messages makes us consciously aware
of the way the ego works to maintain and enhance the
false experience of separation. Once you get to know the
ego's voice, you will recognize it more clearly throughout
the rest of your life and free yourself from believing its
promises.

The following hidden messages are merely examples. As you explore your own knots of suffering, you
will find your own egoic voice, and I guarantee you
that it will be identical or very similar to Cindy's.
Please don't get lost in comparing your list to this list,
because what you find will be perfect for you in the
moment you discover it. Instead, be comforted that
you're not alone and that the cruelty of the messages
doesn't mean there is something horribly wrong with
you. Anyone with an ego (yes, that's right, just about
all of us) is dealing with at least some of these thoughts
and the difficult feelings they engender.

We all share both the dank darkness of the world of
humanity and the brilliant light of the world of divine
truth. Both are here in service to our awakening. When
we listen intently for the hidden messages that have

lived inside our pain, we exhibit the necessary courage to shift our sense of reality. This shift is essential for our happiness and our sanity.

Universal Messages of the Ego, as Received by Cindy (and a Few Billion Others)

- I am not important.
- My feelings are not worthy.
- I am not safe.
- I am not wanted.
- I am abandoned and betrayed.
- I am nothing.
- I deserve nothing.
- I am worthless.
- I must try to be invisible.
- I am embarrassed and ashamed.
- Life is unfair to me.
- I have no support.
- I have no right to breathe.
- I am just taking up space.
- There is no room for me.
- I cannot enjoy wealth.
- I must be a good girl (or boy).
- Everyone rejects me.

- I haven't become anything in life.
- I am wasting my life.
- I hate you, God.
- God hates me.
- Being beautiful/cute/female/male got me molested.
- Death is the way out.
- It's too much.
- I am overwhelmed.
- I am overwhelming to others.
- No one will help me.
- No one cares about me.
- I must be kind and sweet, or else shut up.
- I must have done something horribly wrong.
- I cannot succeed.
- I am heartbroken.

"I must have done something horribly wrong" is one of my personal favorites. As I've gotten more and more aware of my inner process, I've seen how often this thought is at the bottom of any number of emotional experiences. Underneath the anxiety, fear, and self-doubt, this message is almost always at play. I trace this thought back to my very early childhood, and maybe to past lives as well. It has survived over forty-five years and has become an old friend. When this guilt-ridden thought appears, I know right away that I've left my true self, and it signals me to jump in, get wet, and float home to my spiritual connection.

In this list, Cindy uncovered the three universal fears that author Gregg Braden discusses concerning the human condition: fear of abandonment (I'm unlovable), fear of being unworthy (I'm not good enough), and fear of surrender (I can't trust).[16] In addition, the list exposes these cruel thoughts: "I can't be trusted," "I'll never be forgiven," "I'll never feel connection," and "It's hopeless," ending with "I'm helpless and alone. I feel scared, weak, lonely, and afraid of the future."

Whoa—that stuff is nasty! Yet this is the material of the "shadow self," and we must examine it with love and compassion if we're ever going to heal it. Within these self-hating thoughts is what *A Course in Miracles* calls the desire to make a "special relationship," in which the ego reigns over our world. As the *Course* tells us in Chapter 24: The Treachery of Specialness, "Specialness always makes comparisons. It is established by a lack seen in another, and maintained by searching for, and keeping clear in sight, all lacks it can perceive." Through wanting to be special (either especially good or especially bad), we have unconsciously given our egos full control—and we can live in hell because of it.

---

16. Gregg Braden, *Walking Between the Worlds: The Science of Compassion* (Sacred Spaces/Ancient Wisdom, 1997).

Sometimes people ask me, "Why does the ego try to keep us separate? When and why did the ego begin?" These are all great questions, which can lead to some deep discussions. Many philosophers and spiritual teachers tackle them. I choose not to address them, simply because I don't know the answers. Lots of possibilities and theories exist, but that's what they are—just theories. So until Spirit shows me some answers in a way that I'm sure of, I continue to be practical: I forgive.

All Forgiveness Is Self-Forgiveness

When I believe the thought "I must have done something horribly wrong," it's time for me to jump into the river of love, because I need a deep, refreshing drink of healing grace. Here I must choose to separate truth from falsehood because, on a soul level, I have *not* done something horribly wrong. It is not true that I am a guilty, pathetic creature, unworthy of love. Contrary to all the messages I received about my identity as an individual person, at the deepest level I am pure and perfect, the essence of light, just as you are, no matter what you've done or where you've been.

We are all responsible for our actions in life, so correcting our mistakes becomes essential to our peace of mind. As we awaken, we want to reach out with love to people we may have hurt in the world of humanity. Also, in the world of divine truth, as souls we are eternally loved, eternally loving, and wholly at peace. We are created with the same goodness as the Eternal, which cannot create what is not characteristic of its true nature. Since the divine is pure love, then the attributes of creation—of every one of us—are also perfect love.

When we review the list of hidden messages, we see that such harsh thoughts are self-condemning and lead to emotional states of shame, guilt, and fear. Thus, we can see that *all forgiveness is ultimately self-forgiveness,* because, in our minds, we've translated every traumatic event that ever happened to us into a story of self-blame and confusion. Many of the original episodes of fear and pain occurred when we were young children, without much personal power or full development, amplifying our ego's experience that "it's all about me, and it's all my fault."

What is left for us—if we want freedom—is to transform our sick, pitiful self-concept into something of an entirely different order. Since problems cannot be solved on the level of the problem, we must extend ourselves onto a bigger playing field of possibilities and expand into a higher vibration of consciousness.

By leaping into forgiveness, we can transform our inner messages—but only if we examine them to discover what is true and what is false. We must uncover the false ideas that lurk in our minds, masquerading as truth. This is one of the reasons we must find the hidden messages that have lived, perhaps for lifetimes, inside these knots of pain and fear. We need to unmask the pretenders and learn from the whole charade so that we can separate the truth from lies, deceit, and just plain ignorance.

Mind in Matter

There are times when life perfectly mirrors our mind, and if we're paying attention, we'll see the message right in front of our eyes. For instance, Cindy had an amazing experience as she got honest and fearless with herself. This is part of her story, in her own words:

> In working with Ana, many things began to happen with my personal energy as I confronted and healed beliefs in my life. One experience of how my energy changed involved my front doormat. I had been feeling threatened and harassed by my neighbors. I tried to be friends with them, and when it went sour, I had a lot of angry feelings toward them that I buried. I was tired of showing up as the super-"nice" doormat in the world. As my neighborly relations went from bad to worse, the wife of my neighbor would pass by my stoop and kick my doormat! I just knew it was her, even though I'd never seen her actually do it.
>
> One day, when I was really angry with her for writing false accusations about me to our association board, I "threw" all my rage energy at her

through my wall into her house! I had a session with Ana that day and decided not to be a doormat in this world any longer. My life had a much more empowered and greater purpose. When I went for a walk a short time later, I noticed that my doormat had been kicked clear into the bushes! So, I picked it up and threw it in the trash can. There would no longer be a doormat to kick! Later that evening, a moving van arrived, and they moved out. Thank God Almighty. I was done!

Actually, the unpleasant neighbors made another appearance later in Cindy's life, because she wasn't as done as she thought. Throwing rage at people isn't being done with them, and Cindy soon learned that she had plenty more healing opportunities ahead. But the story about the doormat illustrates what I'm exploring here about inner messages. Cindy had an inner message that said, "I am a doormat. I'm here to be walked on. I am unworthy." Finally, she was able to see that thought clearly and decided not to keep giving it her life force. The doormat—literally the way to her front door—became a symbol that she could understand and work with physically. As soon as she threw her doormat into the garbage (both in her mind and in her physical reality), things immediately changed in her life.

Remember what we learned about brain science? Cindy sincerely wanted change, and she used H.O.W. and forgiveness to begin shifting the neural nets within her brain. She also contacted her heart's and cells' intelligence and brought them more and more into coherence. She no longer agreed with the thought "I am a doormat," and this powerfully transformed her outlook on life. She no longer saw herself as helpless, and therefore her entire universe realigned itself to meet her in a new place.

As the scientist Candace Pert said, "Our emotions will literally guide our eyeballs into where they look... We see what we expect to see."[17] Cindy challenged herself to unwind a lifetime of abuse and self-hatred. She changed what she expected to see, and surprising miracles began to occur.

We don't always have such impeccable one-to-one correlations to our inner world showing up on the material plane, but similar dynamics are always at work on the subtler levels of our psyche. So even if you don't have any experiences that are as obvious as Cindy's doormat story, go within to find your hidden messages. It's worth the time and energy, because this step will bring you to freedom, allowing you to release what is not and was never true, and claim the truth instead.

---

17. Candace Pert in *People v. The State of Illusion*, a 2012 documentary by Austin Vickers, directed by Scott Cervine, Exalt Films.

Support for Plunging In

Have you ever taken a dip in a clear alpine lake? I live in the mountains of Northern California, where pristine lakes still beckon during the summer. But let's be clear: in high elevations, that water is freezing! Sometimes it feels like cold fire on my skin. The experience of challenging myself to get in that frigid water and stay in as long as possible is satisfying, though not exactly what I'd call relaxing. To get wet, I need a really hot day, and even then sometimes I splash around shrieking like a maniac for a few seconds and then jump right back out onto the shore. It always feels thoroughly cleansing and well worth the effort.

That's what the journey to find your hidden messages may feel like, especially the first few times you try it. It feels like a plunge, and it may be a very unfamiliar one for you, especially if you've pushed your emotions way down deep to drown out the hidden messages of an entire lifetime (or lifetimes, perhaps). This deep inner listening process is going to take courage, patience, persistence, and bucket loads of compassion. If you don't feel much of that, particularly compassion for yourself, call on your council of teachers, angels, masters, and saints. They can help you feel compassion, as long as you trust that it's possible. Slow down, breathe, find your body, and listen to your pain.

Discover the hidden messages buried within your knots of suffering. Write them down, speak them out loud, or tell them to a trusted friend or counselor. You can get a helpful free download entitled "My Hidden Messages" at www.anaholub.com, which is simply the following outline in digital form.

My Hidden Messages

1. The area of my body that I'm feeling pain or constriction in is_____.

2. As I slow down, breathe deeply, and explore, I offer compassion and love to this place in my body. Gradually, I hear the knot telling me ...

   About myself:

   About other people:

   About how life is:

Remember to observe these thoughts and learn from them rather than battling, protecting, or judging them or yourself. Be content to learn and explore with an attitude of discovery and curiosity.

If the tight place moves to another location, just continue, repeating these steps as you follow your body's wisdom. Keep softening, breathing, opening, and learning!

Chapter Eight

Step Six—Releasing

We must let go. That's great ... but *how*? I have a friend who is a wonderful teacher. When participants in his group sessions ask him how to let go, he throws his bottle of water at them. When they catch the bottle, he says, "Okay, now drop it." The participant lets go of the bottle, and it falls to the floor.

This is an apt physical example of releasing something. But how do we drop something we're attached to through our beliefs and emotions? While our minds may be intellectually able to handle the notion that "it's all an illusion," our emotional bodies are likely to need help releasing something we're really bound up with. We've created neural nets in our brains, habits of the mind, and we must unlearn them to create new neural pathways.

Coping with Anger

If you experience a lot of anger in your life, you will likely find it living within the emotional/physical constriction you found in your body. During your releasing process, it's essential to understand that anger is what is called a "secondary emotion." You feel anger, but it doesn't exist on its own. There are always other beliefs and their corresponding emotions hibernating beneath it.

When you release anger, wait patiently for the underlying emotions of shame, grief, fear, guilt, indignation, helplessness, and hopelessness to arise as well. If you are someone who habitually exhibits anger as part of your lifestyle, I encourage you to get professional help. Raging behavior can be dangerous to you and to those around you (including pets, other drivers, children, lovers, coworkers, and dear Mother Earth herself).

Right now we live in two worlds, although only the divine one is real. This means we must take responsibility for our habits and seek help when we need it. Just as with every other ailment or malady in this world, Spirit can heal you. And there's nothing wrong with getting support along the path. Pray, and you will be guided to the support you need. As *A Course in Miracles* reminds us, "Do not forget today that there can be no form of suffering that fails to hide an unforgiving thought. Nor can there be a form of pain forgiveness cannot heal." (Workbook, Lesson 198)

One thing is certain: if you live with a lot of resentment, chronic irritation, or tension in your daily life, you will find plenty of fertile material to work with on your path of forgiveness. All the more reason to jump into forgiveness with the full power of your sincerity! You can turn the ferocity of your anger into an uncompromising, flaming-with-desire insistence on truth in every moment of your life. This attitude is sometimes called the "warrior for peace," though I don't favor this terminology. Those who float in the river and joyfully cruise on down to the ocean of divine bliss have left behind any identity of being a warrior. We're swimmers, and no longer warriors at all.

In reality, everyone with an intact ego is suffering from delusion and anger. It is usually repressed so that we can "get along" with ourselves, each other, and our constricted life. To avoid the blistering heat of rage and the despair, fear, and grief that lie in wait below it, many of us fall into depression and various forms of addiction. This gives us a self-medicated, numbing buffer layer between our true self as pure light and "normality." We haven't coped with the fact that we left God and betrayed ourselves as blessed beings, so we blindly hang on to our illusions—and get really angry in the process.

Good news! There are ways to release anger safely. If you are a "rager," this is best done with professional support—at least at first, during the learning stages. A safe, nonjudgmental environment with clear boundaries on behavior is essential.

If you have developed the habit of anger, especially in its extreme form of rage, then I suggest you learn to calm yourself down, using breath and centering techniques. You will also need to take good care of yourself and listen to when you need to discharge and recharge with exercise, humor, journaling, time in nature, prayer, and connecting with others. You need to become aware of the thoughts in your mind that trigger your anger. These are self-generated thoughts, which perpetuate the cycle of hostility within you. Taking responsibility for yourself, rather than violently projecting blame and vengeance on your world, is a key lesson for you. Only then will the work of forgiveness be able to take hold in your heart and mind.

If, on the other hand, you are *not* familiar with your anger and have trouble getting in touch with it, then anger-release techniques like pounding a pillow (with your fists, a tennis racket, or a toy wiffle bat) and yelling at the top of your lungs (preferably where you won't disturb others) can be tremendously helpful.

Breathing Exercise for
Relaxing and Calming Down

This breathing exercise is wonderful for choosing to stay calm, or for bringing yourself back into peace after you've become tense or angry. It is often taught in anger management classes. My students in prison have said that this is the most helpful, practical tool they learned. If using this breath technique can help inmates in the messy, violent world of prison, surely it can help you, too.

Focus on your exhale. Begin counting as you breathe. Breathe about half as long on the inhale as the exhale; e.g., inhale for four counts, exhale for eight counts. Feel any stress in your head, jaw, neck, shoulders, arms, and hands, and focus on sending your energy down toward your feet. Doing this will help you include your entire body, emotions, and mind, rather than just recycling tension in your head, neck, and shoulder area. Feel your heart and breathe through the middle of your chest, feeding your physical as well as your spiritual heart with oxygen and life force. Feel the strength of the earth supporting you.

Repeat your relaxing breath as many times as necessary until you begin to calm down. Stay with this breath until you feel an inner shift. You'll find you have more clarity and better decision-making ability after completing the exercise.

Even Nice Girls Get Angry

As someone who was taught to be a "nice girl" for most of her life, I was overjoyed to contact my anger one day when I was in my early thirties. Here's my story.

I had gone to a classical homeopath soon after my father died. I felt sure I had *miasms,* or imbalances and distortions in my emotional field that were genetic or somehow part of my family lineage. Many of my ancestors had died of cancer, and my father's medical case was complicated and indicated an autoimmune disease. I thought it would be a great idea to use homeopathy to clear my connection to the family disease framework. My homeopathist gave me a remedy for this purpose, and within three days I was seething with a rage I'd never felt before. All the pent-up, silenced, terrified anguish of the family tree, throughout untold generations, came boiling up within me.

I noticed that I was yelling at my wonderful daughter a lot, and I was conscious enough to know this had nothing to do with her. Alarmed, I went outside to the backyard to gather some wood for our stove. The chilly late-winter day beckoned me as I began throwing oak and cedar into the wheelbarrow. I felt so much anger running through me, I started using my body to engage the strength of my emotions. I slammed the wood so hard into the wheelbarrow that it bounced out again! I didn't care; I just needed to keep going, to explore what the hell was going on with me. So I stayed out there, reveling in the sound of wood against metal, not getting a thing accomplished except what was true in the moment. The family rage had come to the surface.

As I continued to make an unholy racket in the backyard, I realized that I had never consciously allowed this much anger into my mind and body before. It was scary, but at the same time, it felt like giving birth to something. Just as if I'd been in labor with a child, I was in labor with rage, and I couldn't stop until the waves of birthing were over.

Gradually, I began to enjoy the process. I became aware of the thick, fuzzy layer of denial that I'd been keeping like a heavy lid on top of all this anger, and I could feel my parents' unspoken agreement to keep denial in place within our family dynamic. I could feel the fear of anger itself, and how I had learned from family and society that this dark force was better left hidden in its dank cave—especially for me, a girl. Many layers of conditioning vividly displayed themselves as I pounded those chunks of oak into the wheelbarrow, one after another.

From that day came a deep revelation. Under all that denial, fear, and anger, I found a special gift I never knew was missing. It was my personal power, the kind that shouts, "I want this! I don't like that! I will!" It was the lion's roar I had silenced long ago, erupting out of me with enough force to move mountains. Unveiled at last, this power had been blocked out, hidden behind the massive Coast Range of my family's dysfunction. With its healing force, I'd blown the cover off all the messages I got as a good little white girl growing up in suburban New Jersey: be nice; don't make waves; be submissive, soft, and sweet; and don't make noise!

The rebellious part of my personality began to shine as I reveled in the ruckus I was raising. My *Bam!* power *Wham!* is *Kapow!* mine! YES! I suddenly felt as if I had shed a giant burlap bag and could move with ease. Not only that, now I could see, I could speak, I could make my wishes known to myself and to the world. I had uncovered the freedom of personal expression, so vital to the realization of my newly unleashed, fully empowered self. I reclaimed my individuality with such enthusiasm that it could never be buried that deep again. How do I know this? I could feel it in my gut. This was soul motion, the dance of taking off the veils. I had completed part of my required striptease, and I was ecstatic.

This is the kind of anger release that brings us to healing, rather than the type that recycles over and over again in a self-reinforcing pattern. One form leads to greater joy and inspiration, while the other leads to violence against self, others, and nature. You can easily find out which form you are participating in by examining the "fruits of your actions," as they say in karma yoga. We will not be attached to the fruits, but we *will* note what they are.

Anger release that includes loud yelling, clanging, and bashing can be especially rewarding for those who have repressed anger. It gives them a safe way to explore what is seen as perhaps the scariest thing in all of life. On the other hand, for someone who already has a habit of yelling and pounding, this kind of release should be attempted only with a seasoned professional. This is because the neural nets in your mind are already set in highways of expectation. Thus, to get a different result from the usual, we must get underneath the anger to find out what gifts lie in store for us.

For some, it will be long-buried self-empowerment. For others, it will be deep sadness and vulnerability. Gradually, we will reclaim all aspects of the shadow and offer them to the Holy Spirit, using the steps outlined in this book. Go toward the aspect of anger that seems scariest to you with trust, breath, prayer, and courage. If you go toward the familiar, you can bet that you're merely recycling habitual mental/emotional material, and no soul motion is happening. It's up to you to be honest, open, and willing, to explore with discernment, to find out.

Am I Ready to Let Go?

Earlier, we discussed the limits of our victim and perpetrator stories. They are useful only because they lead us to the emotions we're carrying, and then give us the choice to disprove or retain the illusory thoughts that we hold about life and creation. When we prepare to release, we remind ourselves that holding on to the stories of grievance, blame, fear, and pain will only keep us imprisoned. The past is over. Now we ask ourselves, "Am I ready to let go?"

But how, when we are shot through with attack and defense, denial and protection, can we possibly give our love to the One who gives us life? More accurately, how can we give our love when we ourselves have been the ones who made this situation?

There must be a vent, a release valve, a path we can walk, to wash all this dense vibration out of our energy field. Why am I so certain such a path exists? Because our true nature is not anger and misery. We've built countless layers of darkness around ourselves because we misinterpreted our human situation and thus made error after error—right along with the rest of our human brothers and sisters. This is sometimes called the action of karma. But this is not the final state of affairs. We need release and guidance. We need our teacher, the eternal, ineffable, Divine Spirit.

As striptease dancers, we shed veil after heavy veil from our enlightened consciousness. Oh, baby, take it off! This is the only way that all sense of separation leaves our hearts and our minds. How else can we realize and directly experience the peace of God—that we are Spirit, one with all?

Most of us are in school, working, or parenting, or doing some combination of these. We are not on a path of living for years in a secluded monastery, where we can spend many hours each day in meditation and prayer. Still, you and I are searching for—in fact, *craving*—a way to contact the compassionate nature of the divine. In releasing, we surrender and find the courage to jump into the unknown.

Yes, you're ready to let go.

Step-by-Step Releasing

When you first began the steps, you offered a prayer and created a sacred space. You joined the sacred space that already exists. One reason for doing this was so there would be a place to release *into*. It's time to remember this part of the process—and to trust it with all the willingness of your soul.

You told the story, felt the feelings, identified the knot of constriction, and learned from it. You heard your mind and its addiction to false thoughts that bring you nothing but misery. Now it's time to give it all away.

I want to point out here that it isn't necessary to relive your entire memory of your victim or perpetrator story. You won't gain any more healing by combing through all the gory details once more. Remember, the story is a symbol of your construction of a false separation from God, whether something awful happened to you in the world of humanity, or you did something awful to someone else. I absolutely support you to make things right in the world as much as you can, but this work is about reclaiming the eternal truth of your divine connection. So use the details of the story to contact your emotions, then follow your emotions inside your body to learn about the constriction you made there. Then breathe it out, with all the trust and sincerity you can muster.

Using Your Breath

At this point in your process, your breath is your greatest ally. To unburden yourself, use a long, slow exhalation. Allow the tears, shame, anger, memories, hatred, fear, bewilderment, guilt, and other painful emotions to flow out of your body with your breath. As you breathe out slowly, let your cells unwind. As you breathe in, fortify yourself with courage and determination. At this point, though, the focus is clearly on the exhalation. BREATHE OUT and let the pain out of your heart, mind, and body.

To release, we must trust that there is a place to put the emotions of the underworld that come up out of us. In the past, we've tried using blame to get rid of them, but we only ended up ruminating on them like a cow chewing its cud. Releasing with forgiveness is the opposite of ruminating—it is transforming. Therefore, we must come to the level of Spirit to activate the transformation.

Remember that however you imagine God to be, this is the time to welcome him, her, or the inexplicable, indescribable Oneness even deeper into your experience. If you have a religion, you can bring it to your process, but you don't need a religion. Call the Holy One anything that brings you closer to the warmth of your own soul nature: God, Goddess, Divine Mother, Holy Spirit, Great Spirit, Pure Awareness, or the power and beauty of nature. What's essential is to reach out to a loving force beyond your individual self.

Two Images to Help You Release

At this point, visualization often helps. Use either or both of these descriptive images to support you in your release. Keep in mind that these images are not just comforting ideas, but the truth of Spirit as it sustains you and the world around you.

The Altar

Imagine a sacred altar, complete with a shining candle, a white silken cloth, and flowers. Its energy is pure, eternal, perfect love. It is the altar of the Holy Spirit, the Holy of Holies. Its love is so pristine, nothing that is not loving can exist within its energy field. The altar actually lives eternally in your heart, but for now, visualize it outside yourself so you can lay your burdens down before it, watching as they vanish before the light.

The Pool of Divine Love

Imagine the immensity of divine love as a huge pool or ocean of mercy, compassion, and understanding. It's always beckoning to you, always welcoming and friendly. You could never find its edges, because it expands forever. There's plenty of room for you and anything that comes up within you to release. When you use this visualization, give away all of your suffering, letting it melt into the vastness of divine love, where you float in the sacred space of your prayer. There is room in this sanctified place for every pain you've ever felt and every false belief you've burdened yourself with, over lifetimes of experience.

Whether you choose to use the image of the altar or the pool, or both, you can trust that this place of refuge can withstand the impact of all your fear and grief. Divine love is unchangeable and immovable. It shines continually, no matter what you think or feel. Spirit leads you home to this place, and all you are doing is releasing what you made up during your (temporary) journey into insanity. It's time to go home to peace by letting go completely, into the grace of your true nature.

Whether you use the altar of light or the pool of divine love to help you, the main purpose of releasing is to allow your suffering to arise without judgment. It comes for healing and to teach you about itself. Breathe it out of your heart, mind, and body. Then, it's gone.

Releasing, Breath by Breath

- Reaching deep inside yourself, bring forth honesty, openness, and willingness to go through whatever it takes for you to let go of your unresolved, unforgiven issue.

- With patience and compassion, let all your emotions, sensations, and thoughts about this issue or relationship rise up from deep inside your psyche, your body, and your mind.

- Focusing on your exhale breath, release the suffering from your muscles, your organs, your cell walls, the spaces between cells, your plasma, and your bones.

- Trusting and releasing with your breath, give the knot your love, then let it unwind.

- Let it all flow OUT of your body. Lay pain before the sacred altar and/or offer it into the pool of divine love. Cry if you need to. Tears are good! They're cleansing and they soften your heart.

- Breathe out, let go. Inhale. Exhale, let go. Trust. Inhale. Exhale, let go. Trust. Repeat.

- Open your body, allowing the emotions and images to drip, melt, and vaporize out of you.

- Let go and let the anguish out of your mind, your memories, and your blood. Feel the release move through your hands and feet—every part of you. Just let it flow on out.

- Keep your deep prayer for freedom uppermost in your consciousness as you continue to feel compassion for yourself and everything that happened.

- Let the past out of your mind. It's over. Give it to Spirit. You don't need it anymore.

- Notice how free you are. You can stop or start at any time. No one is forcing you. You do this release because you want it with all your heart and soul. You are choosing this healing NOW.

- Stay focused. Keep going with this releasing process until you feel a shift. There's no need to analyze with your mind or to figure anything out. Just breathe and release until you intuitively feel "I'm done," or "That's all," or "I'm complete with this." Your body will tell you.

When you release, you notice that the other people in the story don't seem evil or scary anymore. They are actors in a scenario that you created as a soul, to help you learn and grow. For instance, Sal, my dance teacher, no longer seemed oppressive to me once I released my fear of him. In my forgiveness process, I changed him from an attacker who hurt me to a dance partner who could fly with me.

Your perception of the people involved in your story changes as you transform through releasing your pain. Dropping all judgment, release your assumptions about them and focus on clearing out the cobwebs in your heart and mind. Remember that all other people are also perfect and innocent at their core, equal to you in love and magnificence (even if they haven't yet shown you these qualities in this lifetime).

The Essential Decision of Release

In many respects, this inner decision to release the pain of your past is the most sacred moment of the forgiveness process. If you can do this, you can handle anything that rolls toward you on the highway of life. According to *A Course in Miracles*, this release is the very purpose of our lives here on Earth; everything else—including all our career goals, service projects, and creative endeavors—is just part of the decoration. Our willingness to join in communion with God requires that we give up the fear we've made in our minds.

By releasing, we remind ourselves that the guilt and shame we felt was never real, because we *never left* the sacred kingdom for an instant. And if this is true for you and me, it must also be true for all the other players in our victim/perpetrator stories. We can't absolve ourselves without extending this same kindness to all our brothers and sisters. We are left naked before the altar. Our only desire: to reclaim our freedom.

Love holds no grievances.

—*A COURSE IN MIRACLES* WORKBOOK, LESSON 68

Calling on Divine Support for Release

In our humbleness and readiness to let go of suffering, we reach out to the entire field of divine consciousness for help. We know we can't heal if just left to our own, small, individual selves. We already tried that, and it didn't work. It'll never work. Our force field is simply too weak when we think we're alone, and thinking we're alone was the root of our problems in the first place.

If you are open to it, call on the Hindu goddess Kali for help when you release. Gods and goddesses in Hinduism are all symbolic of the one God who gives life to everything. Calling on her is like calling on an archangel or a saint.

Reaching out to Kali, an archangel, or a master teacher helps our minds clarify intention, desire, and the goals of our prayers. How can Spirit answer our prayers for peace and freedom if our minds are unclear about the question? How can we walk across the bridge of forgiveness if we don't know which direction to go? Calling on any divine helper, of any religious or cultural background, will support us if we do it for the purpose of taking off more veils of ignorance.

Why call upon Kali? In Hinduism, Kali is one of the names of Lord Shiva's female counterpart. With Shiva, Kali is responsible for the destruction of worlds and also of the old, the decrepit, the dross of existence. This is a very holy job to have, and it is similar to the work of the Buddhist Manjushri and the Judeo-Christian-Islamic Archangel Michael, both of whom carry swords to cut through ignorance and illusion. Kali is the one who, sometimes in a fierce and terrifying form, takes our fears away for us. Terrifying, yes, but only to the ego, because she is a champion of truth. You can call on her unwavering strength and courage in the face of terror and horror, including memories of any traumatic event you've ever experienced.

By the way, angels, masters, gods, and goddesses are *all* symbolic images. In fact, *you and I* are symbolic images, too. Since there is only ONE essence of life, all the "individuals" that arise from it are symbolic of its oneness. Our journey is all about realizing our oneness so that we can enjoy our temporary individuality as the play of *lila,* the passing show of manifestation, as it's called in Sanskrit. Releasing painful illusions and floating in the river of love gives us more room to dance and sing, just as Krishna's *gopis* (devotees) did in ancient India.

If you feel more comfortable calling on Western cultural images to help you, you can release with Shekinah, the divine feminine principle of Judaism. Shekinah, the

"Presence," brings the essence of holiness to all aspects of life. If you are Christian (or like me, someone who is attuned with Jesus), you can ask Jesus for his support, and his blessing will be with you. In my experience, the Holy Spirit, Shekinah, and Jesus all share the same sacred vibration, except that the Holy Spirit and Shekinah are formless, and Jesus has a historical form. If you are a Muslim, you can reach out to Allah and the angels for support. If you're Buddhist, ask for the wisdom of the Buddha and the compassion of Tara to be with you. The teaching of forgiveness and its bridge to peace are always open to everyone, no matter what religion, race, or background. So reach out for divine help and it will come.

Chapter Nine

Step Seven—
Witnessing the
Changes

After you've released the pent-up thoughts and emotions in your body, examine how you feel. Do you feel lighter, brighter, more in touch with the truth of yourself? Do you sense an openness and clarity that weren't there before? If you sincerely let go during step 6, you will feel different now. Something fundamental within your cell structure and your spiritual vibration will have shifted.

What changes have occurred? If you don't feel anything new, ask yourself to be honest about how much you really allowed yourself to release. Perhaps you can reach deeper, let go even more. If necessary, go back to step 6 and do it again until you feel some kind of movement inside. Keep breathing deeply and slowly, and inquire within.

The PAUSE

Once you feel completely done with releasing, you'll notice a pause. It is the moment between the exhalation and the inhalation, between the inhalation and the exhalation. It is pure, timeless space. Nothing is happening.

This is the emptiness of the Buddha. It is entirely still, full, and quiet within itself. Rest here for as long as it feels right.

I've found that this pause is one of the easiest times for me to become aware of emptiness. See for yourself if you feel this is true for you as well. The more you practice awareness and explore the pause, the more you can catch its presence at other moments in your life. Once you have a sense of what it feels like, you can recognize it and enter it with ease during day-to-day activities.

Note: even though this written section on the pause is brief, it is still vitally important. The section is short because words don't do it justice. You enjoy the spacious simplicity of the pause because for a moment or more, your mind has stopped. During its stillness, you touch true yoga, defined in the first yoga sutra as "the cessation of the modifications of the mind" (*Yogash chitta vritti nirodhah*, in Sanskrit).

To keep things simple, just make sure that when you complete your release, you watch for the pause. It will teach you more than a whole lifetime of book learning.

Examining Your Body

Next, return to the physical place in your body where the knot resided. What's happening there now? Has something changed? Because of your release, your deep exhale, and your trust in the altar of light and the pool of divine love to help you, you should feel different sensations in your body at this point. After all, your conscious decision to release opened up your cell membranes and unbound the energy in the area of constriction. You actually let your tale of woe out of your blood and bones, creating space for deep soul healing to occur.

Scan your body to sense where to go next. Layers of knots often want to release in the same session. If you felt and released tightness in your belly, for instance, and it feels more open and relaxed, find out if there is now another place that feels tense—perhaps in your heart, throat, shoulders, or head. Sometimes you'll release an obvious spot (such as in a knee or ankle where there was a past injury) and then notice that your gut or other body areas want attention. Simply follow your body's wisdom. It knows where to go and when. You're finally listening to it! Just keep going. If there is another area, focus your attention on it and repeat steps 3 through 6 to continue your forgiveness process.

It's worth mentioning here that it doesn't matter whether, during a given session, you unwind one knot or many. Each session will be different, offering you specific guidance and teachings in the moment you need them. Please resist comparing one session to another. One time might be very dramatic, tearful, or full of soul messages. Another may be much more subtle, perhaps less emotional, but you find that you integrate its wisdom into your life in a new and mystical way. Let the dance happen in just the way it needs to, without placing extra layers of judgment and assumptions upon it. Take the layers off. Be as innocent as a child. Ask. Listen. Learn. Let Spirit teach you in the ease and perfect timing of the Holy Instant. Nothing is missing.

Possible Changes after Releasing

Your body will let you know immediately how it's changing. If you haven't yet developed a refined connection with your physical body, this is a great way to begin. If you already feel deeply attuned to your body, you'll become even better at it as you delve into quiet alignment with its rhythms. Checking in with the changes will enlighten you on a whole new level, as each moment becomes a messenger with fresh information.

After releasing with this forgiveness process, clients often report feeling lighter, more open and peaceful. Specifically, the area where the constriction lived, perhaps for decades, now transmits a profoundly new energetic vibration. The images of heavy darkness, fiery anger, or writhing snakes no longer register in the body, emotions, or mind. It's quite incredible to witness and even more satisfying to experience firsthand.

These changes happened for me during a phase in my life when past lovers began showing up unexpectedly, either in dreams, in person, or by e-mail. Over the course of a few months, I reconnected with my daughter's father, whom I hadn't seen in six years. I also got an e-mail from my first boyfriend in high school (a real blast from the past), and reached out to an old friend who was like a long-lost brother to me. By cooking up these synchronicities for me, Spirit was inviting me to look at the way I felt about men. I knew something big was up, so I was on the lookout for a potential release and the peace it brings.

One day during this time, I attended a yoga class. My body felt warm and strong, and my breath flowed full and alive. Holding a challenging pose, I suddenly became aware of an intense energetic knot deep in my lower belly. Its colors and textures were dark and very dense, kind of like a black hole. Black holes are incredibly dense; they have such a strong gravitational field that they suck in all light and matter around them. The spot was tiny, but astoundingly potent. I'd never felt anything like it before.

I kept my focus on this new place in my body as the class moved along and I moved with it. Later that day, I sat down, quieted my mind, and prayed for insight. "What do I need to know about this spot?" I asked. "What thoughts and emotions live here?" Revisiting my belly, I tuned in, sensing this was connected with the men of my past. The first wave of feeling was disappointment. Yes, I'd surely felt that in my intimate relationships. Breathing slowly, I took another look. Something else lurked beneath the disappointment. What could it be?

Then it hit me. Bitterness. The black intensity of the knot matched perfectly with a sense of deep, bitter pain. Its texture changed and became hard, rocky, and metallic. Finding that spot was like discovering a gunshot wound that I'd been too numb to feel before that moment. It seemed like I'd found a bullet lodged in my womb. And I knew who had put it there: me.

All the disappointment of my entire life as a girl and woman lived in that spot, pressurized like a fossil until it was hard as a rock. One disappointment mixed with another, and another, and more and more; it magnified my pain over decades until I turned it into bitterness.

There it hid, my personal tyrannosaurus rex gallstone of love relationships, becoming blacker and denser over time, pulsing deep within my subconscious mind. This black place represented bitterness not only in this lifetime, but my soul's karma throughout millennia. I knew I needed to release it, to forgive all the stories related to it, and to finally find balance and peace.

Surprisingly, because this wasn't my usual style, I waited for a few days before setting up my forgiveness session. I needed to keep the black hole a while longer, just to contemplate it. I knew that giving it over to divine love was inevitable for me, but I wanted more time to sit with it, to get to know its bitterness. I needed to taste its black density and feel its concentrated power before I could let it go.

A few days later, I sat in meditation once again. This time, I felt ready for release. I realized that giving up this pain would change something fundamental about my life. I'd lived with my suffering for so long, it almost felt like I'd be giving up a familiar friend (even though its energy was far from friendly). I had no idea who I'd be without it, but I knew it had to go.

I opened with a short prayer and set my sacred space. Breathing consciously, I began exhaling directly from deep within my belly, letting compassion soften the edges around the knot. Waves of memories came to me and tears flowed through me, and I gave them all to the Holy

One for healing. I lay down my burdens before the altar of divine love.

All the frustration, hopelessness, and helplessness I'd ever felt regarding boys and men poured out of me in a rush of emotion: the times when I'd loved so deeply but felt unseen, unappreciated, or betrayed; the times when I'd tried so hard to express myself to my lover but couldn't seem to get through to him, and crashed into a wall of confusion and pain instead; the moments of sadness when I'd felt the end of our love approaching and I couldn't change it or fix it ... all this came tumbling out.

My personal feelings and experiences rose up for release, and in addition, I saw cultural conditioning coming up, too. I knew intellectually that the stories I'd been told as a child weren't true. Emotionally, though, I still had an expectation that each boy or man I loved was somehow supposed to transform into some sort of prince on a white horse. He'd come and save me, scooping me up and taking me away to his palace ... where everything was safe and secure. We're taught in many cultures that romantic love is the highest form of love. When egos get messy and the whole relationship seems to go to hell in a handbasket, we can become disappointed and, eventually, bitter. Our hearts shrivel and no longer want to trust. I found all this inside my body as I let it go with my soul's sincerity, giving it to the One.

This phase of release was intense, but it didn't take long. In a matter of a few minutes, I'd let go of a lifetime's worth of anguish. I returned my attention to the knot. "What changes had occurred there?" I wondered. Focusing on my lower belly once again, I watched a transformation take place: what had been a dark, almost malevolent place now moved and pulsed, turning from dense black obsidian into a fount of vitality. What had once pulsed in bitterness became an energy that was free to dance and travel. Amazed, I witnessed this life force turn into what felt like an elixir of red wine. It quickly traveled through my blood and merged with my physical and spiritual bodies. I felt completely renewed and rejuvenated, as if someone had just handed me a sacred tonic of the highest vibration.

Because I gave my pain to the Holy Spirit, my suffering disappeared. What seemed so impenetrably difficult or hopeless transformed into a new, open place of wonder. My prayer of gratitude welled up in soft tears of joy and relief. All that remained was a blessed feeling of inner peace and soul satisfaction. The hard work for the session was complete, and my cup runneth over.

This new feeling demonstrates the power of spiritual love. Romantic love can be beautiful, but sacred love binds us together eternally. It heals anything and everything that we give to it with a clear intention.

I don't introduce this idea of transformation to you without asking you to examine it for yourself. Find out. As you explore this forgiveness path and let it spread throughout every memory and vision of the future, you will absorb its sparkling truth directly. The river always goes to the sea. In our case, it's the sea of peace, wisdom, and joy.

Chapter Ten

Step Eight—
Examining
the Lessons

When you feel intuitively that you are finished releasing (at least for now), tune in again. Rest in the stillness and enjoy it. This is vacation time for your mind. Let yourself float for as long as it feels right. *Aaaaahhhhh.*

Once the painful emotions have been released from your body-reservoir, you'll notice that there is now room to explore your soul themes and lessons.

When you are ready, it's time to ask, "What's the point? At a soul level, why did I have this experience on Earth? What do I need to learn from this story? What can I be grateful for?"

All you need is some helpful guidance so you can recognize the lessons awaiting you. When you see the teachings and witness them as truth, something very deep inside you will relax. Your soul has been waiting for this moment to put aside falsehood and fear. You will feel ready to expand upon your understanding of the differences between the ego and Spirit's wisdom. You are now ready for peace.

The Ego Is Obvious

Fortunately, the ego works in a very obvious and un-creative way. By now, you're probably at a stage in life where you can recognize the way it works, at least some of the time. This is why *A Course in Miracles* speaks about what the ego "makes" as opposed to what God creates. Since the ego's mission is maintaining a false sense of separation (and corresponding emo-tional states of alienation, loneliness, despair, and fear), we can easily recognize where we've been allow-ing the ego to lurk within our minds.

The mind without ego is a holy thing, constantly poised in readiness to serve the One; the mind with an ego is simply full of errors, which may be corrected by Spirit at any time. Finding the errors and breathing out the pain (steps 3–6) is a necessary activity so that we can allow room for our soul lessons to reach our mind. Now it's time to go after buried treasure.

Embracing the Opposite

Every emotional knot has a message or messages—hidden wisdom waiting for us. You found the first few layers of messages earlier, in steps 2 and 5. Remember Cindy (and you, and me) and our long list of self-hating thoughts? Those were some rough waters!

Then you used H.O.W. to release—you were honest, open, and willing. You breathed the fear, pain, and sorrow out of your body. Since you let the fear message out, you made room to let the love message in. At this point, you're ready to listen even more deeply to the underlying soul messages that will heal your mind and heart.

Sit Quietly and Receive the Wisdom

Sit quietly and become aware of yourself as a totality—spirit, mind, emotions, and body. Allow your inner wisdom to touch you and teach you. New insights will emerge from your spiritual intelligence. These are important keys for your soul's understanding, so take some time to let them come to you. In other words, don't search for them or *do* anything; just allow. Breathe. Rest in the emptiness. Enjoy the simplicity. See how the jewels of wisdom come of their own accord. You will notice that they contain messages that are opposite from the ones you held for so long.

For instance, what message did I receive after I let go of all that bitterness around my relationships with men? My victim story began like this: "I can't trust men. They will eventually betray or disappoint me. My prince will never come. I feel disappointed and bitter." Some of the hidden messages, which arose after I took responsibility for my feelings, were these: "I can't trust myself in love. I've totally screwed up (in the past). I'll make terrible mistakes (in the future). I can't trust my own judgment." Hmmmm. I detect a theme here. You may recognize it, too, because it's one that a lot of us share: trust. Trust in relationships with others, with ourselves, and with Spirit.

The opposite messages I received once my release was complete were these: "I *can* trust. I can trust love itself. I am love. I love love!" At this point, my preoccupation with men (i.e., attachment to romantic love) dropped away and I focused on my direct connection to life, pure awareness, and my simple happiness. As long as I remained true to these positive, supportive messages, my vibration changed and I could fully enjoy my connection with men. And although I'd had lots of friendships and some deep communion with men before that point, my sense of peace within myself and my relationship with others truly blossomed after I received these teachings.

Spirit offers you profound realizations. Just as I did, you can learn to trust yourself, your intuition, what life brings you, and life itself. *How different your inner peace will be if you choose to trust!* How much deeper your visions will go if you trust your Spirit and its holiness! Your decision-making process will be completely revolutionized. Trust: one word, yet a most powerful message.

Another example of receiving soul guidance could stem from any kind of need for self-love. Most of us could enjoy a lot more of that! Without self-love, we have little to give anyone else. When I withheld love from people in male bodies, I withheld it from myself, because I stopped the flow of love through me. Also, because we are all One, and in truth there is only one person appearing as many, if I didn't feel love for male folk (or anyone), I didn't feel love for myself. If you've withheld love from others, you've withheld it from yourself, too. This means that by now, we both know all about living with the results of withholding love: despair, loneliness, apathy, and perhaps addiction. (Remember, there are also subtle as well as obvious manifestations of our suffering.) It's time to forgive ourselves, love ourselves, and turn our thoughts around.

Once you've released the emotional pain you were holding, there's room for messages of wisdom to rise up within you. Listening deeply, you might hear Spirit within you say, "Love yourself." It won't sound cheesy or insincere. In fact, you'll get the teaching on a profound level that will go straight to all your cells, emotions, thoughts, and memories. It will infuse you with a warm wave of blessing. If you respect and care for it, this teaching will uplift you for the rest of your life.

The lessons coming from Spirit may be simple. Try not to be disappointed if the wisdom that bubbles up seems too brief or plain. Simplicity is beautifully elegant, and the message will always be tailored to your needs in the moment. Once you get the hang of this, the accuracy of the opposite message will strike you to your core. This is what you've wanted to know all along, yet the world handed you an entirely different set of circumstances and alternate realities! At first you believed the *maya*, or illusion, but now you are exploring ever deeper into truth. You are raising your vibration as you uncover and receive the gems—the fruits of your quest!

The Three Fears—Turned Around

As we discussed in chapter 7, the three universal fears are interconnected, powerful ideas that inform your first layer of hidden messages. They make up the gooey soup of your neediness and misery. To review, the three core fears are fear of abandonment (I'm unlovable), fear of being unworthy (I'm not good enough), and fear of surrender to God (I can't trust). The three fears give rise to additional neurotic thoughts that try to steal our peace of mind: "I can't be trusted," "I'll never be forgiven," "I'll never feel connection," "It's hopeless," and "I'm helpless and alone. Therefore, I feel lonely and I'm afraid of the future." (Are we having fun yet? Yikes!)

What happens when we turn those fears around and look at them from a Oneness point of view?

Since you've released the pent-up anger and fear that you made up around the false idea that "I'm not good enough," there is now room to receive the wisdom of the *true* idea that "I am holy." Notice that I didn't say the opposite is "I am good enough." Why? Tune in to that statement. It's still right there on the battlefield. Tension still exists there because of a split in the mind. Good enough? For what? For whom? Until when? To walk off the battlefield altogether, we have to move to a completely different perspective.

As *A Course in Miracles* reminds us, love has no opposite. Here we get to witness this truth in action, within our own hearts and minds. The true statement that corresponds to healing the core fear that "I'm not good enough" is the realization that "I am holy." This is simply an honest statement about the real nature of every being who was ever created.

Now you can see why you're not special! Instead, you are holy. You are the Christ essence, and so am I. So is everyone in your victim/perpetrator story. We can't hide from our collective true nature. This is our identity, as it is given to us by our Creator. It has nothing to do with being good enough or not good enough. Once we rest in this, we've left the battlefield. We have found peace.

Let's try this exercise again with the core fear that "I am unlovable." To raise yourself out of the mire of lies about this one, you search for the highest vibration of truth you can find. One thought could be that "I am lovable." This statement is true. What's another true statement about love? How about "I am love"? This is an even more direct passage into the holy relationship that lives forever within you. Your very nature is love! How could you have thought you were unlovable when, in fact, you're oozing love from your heart and mind eternally?

Yes, in the world of humanity, we've hidden our true nature from ourselves and each other under untold layers of generational pain. We've also been trained to look outside for another person to complete us. We were taught to search for one of the pinnacles of human experience: romantic love. Then, in forgiveness, we are reminded by the Holy One that *we are love!* No one is left out, no one is excluded—everyone is equal, pure, and innocent in the truth of divine love.

Let's examine the last fear, the fear that you can't trust. It's a fear of surrender, a fear of the power of the One. With this fear comes a whole host of sub-fears, like fearing that you've done something horribly wrong and that you're guilty and can never fix your mistake. You fear that since Spirit is not made of love, you'll never be forgiven for your errors, and your whole life is hopeless. Trusting and letting go seem dangerous, as if you'd die if you did so. Actually, your ego will die if you do so. (Remember, these fears are often subconscious. If you look deeply, you'll find this fear. It is central to maintaining an ego.)

To turn this one around, first you must let go of the fear and trust instead, as you did when you released in step 6. Here you take trust deeper, because you consciously embrace and welcome it. You recognize that you'll get no further on the path without it. Fear that you can't trust turns into its opposite with this realization: "I CAN trust. In fact, I make the choice to trust beyond what I can see, taste, touch, hear, and feel. Beyond my senses, there is a different sort of information available, but only if I surrender, giving everything to my Creator." With this intense willingness to let everything go, you make room for pure love.

By surrender, I don't mean that you need to stay on the battlefield and wave a white flag, signifying that you're the "loser." That's the old, ego-centered model of surrender. This kind of surrender is entirely different. It's a spiritual experience of the highest order, requiring prodigious soul-strength. It is a fundamental offering of your entire self to God consciousness.

The whole path of forgiveness can be seen as a path of surrender. We're letting everything go that isn't love; we're letting it drop to the ground. We feel the intensity of our desire for freedom from separation and despair. We welcome truth and love with every breath. This path is a fundamental, foundational meditation, one that turns into an artistic masterpiece for each one of us, coming forth organically as we live our daily lives.

Learning Your Soul Lessons

Listening deeply, you'll begin to hear your essence speaking to you with wisdom. Stay with this process, and note all the intuitive messages that come up for you. Some will be general, such as "I can trust now," and some will be specific to the situation of your forgiveness story. For instance, in healing my relationship with my mother, I saw Mom's illness and suicide as a way to release my fear of insanity and grow in trust and compassion. The entire situation compelled me to deepen my devotion to my Divine Mother.

There will be many "turn-arounds" where you will see how much you projected your own fears onto other people and events. Happily, you'll see how the whole scenario was a perfect set-up for your healing.

Ask yourself the following questions to support your inner listening. Answers will rise up naturally, without effort, and they'll always be encouraging and compassionate. If you begin to hear any negativity, this is a sign that there's more to release. No problem! Just breathe, trust, and release the pain. Many layers may come for healing in one sitting. Stay with the process until only positive messages come to you.

It's very helpful to write down your realizations, either in the moment or later on. If you'd like a digital version of the following questions, go to www.anaholub.com for a free download. You can print it out and fill in the blanks. It contains these questions:

- What hidden messages from my soul come to light after release?
- Why or how did my soul need this situation?
- Can I see perfection in the situation?
- What strengths, realizations, and compassion do I now have because I've gone through this session and forgiven?
- How can I be grateful for what happened?

Chapter Eleven

Step Nine—
Soul Expansion

You'll be happy to find out that by step 9, you've reached the dessert course of the forgiveness meal. Early in the process, in building up to step 6 (release), you worked to honestly feel the pain and fear that was lodged within your victim story. The release itself was such a deep opening; your emotions poured through you as you offered them to the One. Then you calmly opened to the messages you were ready to receive. After all this, there's nothing left to do but infuse yourself with love, light, and grace. That's why soul expansion tastes so sweet.

Deepening the Pause

First, check within to find out if any additional layers of fear arise. If you honestly don't feel anything tap-tap-tapping at your consciousness for healing, then just relax. Don't force yourself into more processing, just for the sake of processing. There's no need to push or strain. When you're done, you're done, and you'll know it.

You will notice that you've gotten very, very quiet inside, not only about your forgiveness issue, but about everything. Nothing is going on. Everything seems simple and still. Enjoy this profound simplicity. It is the pause between the exhale (all the releasing you just did) and the inhale (upcoming dessert). Stay here as long as you like. Usually, this is a fairly brief period of time (one to five minutes). If you hang out here too long, you'll probably begin to space out and you may forget to go on to step 9, which is a crucial part of the forgiveness process. So stay here for a few minutes, noticing your breath as it easily floats in and out of you. Gradually, you'll feel a natural desire to begin breathing more deeply. This is your signal that your expansion has begun.

Drinking IN with Enjoyment

I name this part "dessert" because all the goodness and joy that's been shut out of your life has a chance to enter you now. This happens without effort, but it becomes most potent when done consciously, so make sure you remain very present. For this section, focus on your INHALE breath.

It's helpful to remember your circle of cosmic supporters at this time. If you invited masters, angels, or other helpers in your opening prayer, acknowledge them now. Together, you will all engage in drinking in the very essence of life.

Once you've made contact with the beings in your sacred circle, begin to use your inhale breath to fill yourself with divine love. Open up by reaching energetically to connect with the heavens above the crown of your head. In the space above your head, feel a doorway open and invite light to pour down through you. Open your feet and receive blessings from the earth as well. Let the vitality of life enter you on all levels. Tune in to your heart, including the back of your heart. Make sure you allow the light to fill every crevice of your being.

*With every inhale, **drink in** the light.*
*With every exhale, **relax**.*

Allow the grace of the One to enter you with its subtle, healing power. All you need to do is say, "Yes, come on in!" and the wisdom of the life force will do the rest. Feel its holy presence as it makes its way through all of your blood, bones, memories, dreams, and desires. Pay special attention to any places in your physical body that served as reservoirs for suffering. ALLOW the light to infuse these places now, with full willingness and gratitude.

Sometimes it's fun to play with colors at this stage. You may spontaneously feel guided to focus on different hues of light, such as gold, white, pink, violet, or any other healing color. Do this only if it feels easy and in the flow—in other words, don't get into your mind or begin other meditation practices. Let the colors come if they do. If not, don't worry about it.

Continue to fill up with pure light. Trust that this light knows exactly what to do to bring healing to you. Just receive on the inhale and relax with every exhale. There's nothing to do but enjoy the goodness of life.

Your circle of supportive light beings reminds you that we never wake up alone. We do it together, because our very nature is love in communion with itself. So we are always completely connected. You'll FEEL the reality of this during your soul expansion now.

Inhaling grace is like drinking the best, most delicious and healing milkshake in the world. PULL its radiance into you, as if you're a child who's trying a chocolate shake for the very first time. Be in wonder, gratitude, and eagerness to get some more! This is totally fine, because you'll soon realize that drinking this divine nectar is thoroughly beneficial to your soul. You actually FEED yourself on its wisdom and power. With a deep sigh of relief, you begin to comprehend that nothing you can do will change the eternal potency of this light. Its purpose is to heal and fulfill you. You can never run out, and you lack for nothing. Everything is given in every holy instant. Nothing is missing, and everything is included in the sacredness of this moment. Your soul comes to rest. Peace is yours. Drink some more.

If you don't feel much at this point, simply go deeper into trust. You did not make yourself; you were created by the One. The holiness that created you will not leave you now, or ever. It's up to you to sink into the Oneness field with faith in something much vaster than your individual self. Pull on the help of your team, because that's what your helpers are there for. Keep going until you feel completely saturated with divine love.

Note: If you are reading this for the first time and haven't done the full forgiveness process yet, you may begin to worry that you won't be able to "do it right." "Oh no!" your ego whispers. "What if I fail?"

Do your best to ignore this voice. Rest assured that after you've done the inner work with honesty, openness, and willingness and released the pain that bound you, this stage feels absolutely delightful. It's the whipped cream with the cherry on top. It's the vacation you always wanted, the beach in Tahiti, the ultimate fly-fishing trip, the reward and recognition your ego sought in a million other ways (which never worked). Here is the blessing for real. It brings you directly to the peace of your own heart. Everyone knows how to do this step intuitively. Nothing could be more natural.

It's ESSENTIAL to Receive

Perhaps, like me, you've had times when life seemed to be a trial by fire, a crazy succession of one crisis after another. If so, receiving peace may not feel easy at first. This isn't because receiving is difficult, it's because you've made a habit of traveling from mini-disaster to major trauma, then going back to mini-disaster again. This pattern describes what you think of as "life " (e.g., "Life is difficult and unfair"), so the simplicity and ease of receiving pure light can seem disconcerting. Never mind. Just receive anyway. Your soul already knows how to do it, and in truth, you're actually craving the true essence of love with every aspect of your being.

Notice with honesty if you want to cut this part of the process short. I've had more than one client who could muster up plenty of emotion and release with gusto, but then wanted to get up and leave! Don't abandon the party without dessert! The night is young and the band just started. Your favorite music is playing— don't you hear it? Sit for a spell. Get comfortable. Feed yourself deeply. For God's sake … for your sake … don't miss out on the best part!

Just as we have little training in Western society for emotional honesty and letting go, we haven't been given much guidance for receiving the grace of the One.

There aren't many maps, so we just need to find out for ourselves what it feels like in our physical bodies, emotions, and thoughts. In this step, we bring Spirit into matter. This is a sacred path. Stick with it and contact your mystical nature directly. No one needs to teach you this part. Just let it happen.

Rewiring Your Entire System

As we explored in chapter 1, this forgiveness process unkinks your neural nets and forms new pathways for synaptic information to flow. It happens in your brain, and just as importantly in your heart, and continues throughout your physical, emotional, and mental bodies. Finally, you become consciously linked with Spirit.

By deeply receiving the nectar of light during step 9, you complete the exchange program you began with God. Drinking in the purity of original spiritual intelligence, you feed your cells with new information. Life is no longer difficult, demeaning, and cruel. Instead, life is a gift: golden, sacred, and supportive to you and your happy dreams.

By receiving the truth of life, you see that the basic nature of all creation is good. It is human misunderstanding and distortion that lead to sorrow and suffering in this world. Even the most difficult life situations can be seen in a new light, if you open to the possibility that we live more than once, and every lifetime gives us myriad chances to realign with the beauty of creation. Through challenge and experience, we uplift our lives and connect back to the power and glory of the One—but only if we choose it. Your willingness to receive is a potent aspect of this reconnection. Honor it, and find out how much the divine honors you!

Note: Whenever you've finished releasing and you've rested in emptiness a bit, you can drink in the light. It may help you to look deeper as you open to receive wise messages, and it will fortify you if additional pain arises and you need to release some more. The order of the steps is logical, but there's also some flexibility because your entire process occurs in the spontaneity of the moment. Just remember that we need to let go to make room for bliss. Trying to get to joy by jumping over your pain (i.e., without forgiving/letting go) will never be a successful plan.

Expanding the Sacred Circle

Once you feel completely full of life-giving light, stretch further in your receiving to become *absolutely saturated* with it. Begin to overflow; be a FOUNTAIN of divine love. Feel a rich cocoon of golden essence gently bathing your whole body with peace and relaxation. Light fills you and emanates from you, giving you a tangible aura glowing all around as well as within you.

*When you fill yourself in this way, you realize at last that **there is nothing to forgive**. What was needed was your offering to the Holy Spirit in the form of deep re-*

lease. You needed to cleanse the suffering of your heart and mind because it stood in the way of you and God. Whatever you or others did in your forgiveness scenario is gone. Your upset around it is gone, too. What's left is the wisdom gained from the lessons of your experience. What's left is your gratitude to your Creator for giving you the preciousness of your life and EVERYTHING that happened. What remains is your love for every being who played a part in your awakening.

You thought you needed to forgive, and found out that forgiveness in the traditional sense, in the end, is also an illusion...a helpful one, but nonetheless not real. Why? Because each holy instant is perfect. There is no other way to peace but to accept this and relax into it.

Bring to mind all of the divine beings you invited to the circle at the beginning of the process. Give thanks for them and their pure support of your enlightenment. They are present with you as your sacred community. Your circle is REAL.

You are overflowing with love, and there is no end to the glory you've received. The only thing to do now is to share this love for the benefit of all beings. It's time to welcome more people, to expand the love and give it away. Start by speaking out loud the names of any additional friends and allies you'd like to invite energetically to your circle. There is no need to search your memory or work at it in any way; just let the impressions of people (and others, like ancestors, pets, or nature spirits) naturally arise. Whoever wants to join you on a spirit level will come forward easily in the form of a prompting in your mind or an image of his or her face.

As I've grown more familiar with doing this work, I find more openness to invite new and different people. For example, now that my heart is clear of my memories and lessons from both my parents, I can invite them as beloved ancestors. Sometimes I feel the presence of another elder who passed on in recent years. I'm grateful to feel her support as I invite her to my circle.

Your circle is your spiritual celebration, so invite whoever shows up. Let the beings arrive into your mind, then let them in with gratitude. Speak their names one by one.

Everyone who comes to the circle arrives in his or her spirit body. They aren't weighed down by their personalities, and neither are you. This point is crucial for your understanding, because when souls meet in their purity as children of the One, there is no rancor, no regret, no guilt or shame between them. Your part in any misunderstanding has been given—by you—to the One for cleansing. Once you become filled with light, only the light will come to meet you in your circle.

After you've extended invitations to your allies and welcomed them to the sacred council, you may also choose to welcome the people who played difficult parts in your forgiveness story. Only do this step if you feel ready. You'll know. These things can't be forced. If you aren't ready this time, repeat the process sometime in the near future and eventually, you'll recognize the need to go all the way to the heart of God WITH the brothers and sisters in your story.

Mary's Story

For example, a client named Mary came to me after an intense and troubled relationship. At first, she told me her partner was mostly to blame, but soon she also took responsibility for her delusions. During our session, she realized how much of her own pain she'd dumped onto her partner, and how the whole relationship had been based on the "bumper-car effect" of two people projecting their fears onto each other. They'd come close, then violently bounced off the edges of their own terror, like bumper cars at a carnival.

Mary felt a lot of sorrow and shame about how incredibly helpless she'd felt with her man (e.g., obsessively texting, yelling, threatening, throwing things, etc.) when all she really wanted was to come close, be intimate, and grow spiritually. She saw clearly how these patterns did not begin with this relationship, but began in early childhood and perhaps spanned into previous lifetimes. She truly wanted to heal and uplift this textbook example of a "special" relationship by transforming it into a holy one.

With deep sincerity, Mary released her fear and shame with breath and prayer. She imagined the altar of Spirit and laid down her burdens. She rested in stillness, then filled herself with light, learning the lessons her soul had gathered for her. By the time she entered step 9, Mary was ready to energetically invite her sweetheart, Mark, into the circle. Tears of relief washed through her as she retained the light and kept it holy, and at the same time invited Mark to witness her in her soul's beauty. These two had rarely given each other a glimpse of their true selves during their turbulent relationship. Now, Mary claimed her soft strength and spoke to Mark with love and tenderness.

I encouraged her to speak aloud to Mark's Presence. First, she welcomed him by name. "Welcome to our circle, Mark." Next, she told him of her gratitude for him as a soul. "I love you, Mark. I'm sorry for any pain I caused, for all the craziness. Thank you for your love! I wish you only the very highest and best. I also know we need to part. I need to move on, and I think you know you need to move on, too. We'll always be connected. Go with God, dear brother. Be happy in the light!"

With a deep breath, Mary let go of the form of her relationship to Mark, and simultaneously kept hold of her love and eternal communion with him. She felt an enormous burden dropping away, and a wonderful sense of inner peace replacing it as she showed Mark her true self. In reality, she showed *herself* her true self, and invited Mark's soul to witness it with her. When she did that, she could feel the linkage of Spirit that lives inside her and Mark and everyone. On the deepest level, there is only one person—the Oneness that lives within every being.

Witnessing with Love— Being Witnessed in Love

Like Mary, at this point in your process you'll feel tremendous peace and joy. Your soul is doing the work it came to do in this lifetime, and it feels immensely satisfied. Coming into reconciliation by learning the lessons of Spirit opens your heart to grace. Enjoy it, and share it with all of the beings in your circle.

If there is anything else you'd like to do or say to the person you've invited to your circle—such as bow, put your hands into a prayer position over your heart, or silently send love—do so now. Repeat the steps of energetic invitation and communication with any people who are involved, including your parents or others who helped you work out this pattern at an earlier stage.

There's no limit to the number of people you can spiritually invite to your sacred circle. That said, there's no need to fill up the space. *Only invite those who belong there.* It may be only one person, or perhaps you'll keep the circle sacred with just you and your team of mystical helpers. Know that your forgiveness of yourself and others won't be complete until you can invite the biggest "perpetrators" of your story and welcome them with love. Keep going until you can get to this point, even if it takes you several sessions to get there.

Every being who enters this sacred space is an equal, eternal child of God. You'll really feel this truth at this point in the process. The teachers of the most high, the angels, the ancestors, and the "adversaries" of your past commune without any problem whatsoever, the way the leaves on an oak tree live in harmony with each other. We are all one, the way all our cells are one within our body.

Witness everyone in the circle as the most precious being who ever existed, because they are. Keep the light within you, and see it in others. You are practicing now for a lifetime of ease and harmony with the world. As you think, so it is.

As you let this feeling of peace sink in, you'll feel your cell walls and neural nets adjusting to a new vibration. You are teaching yourself about holy relationship, and making a soul choice to live this way from now on. You have chosen to end the cycle of pain that affected you and your entire community. Now you step into a whole new way of being.

Chapter Twelve

Step Ten—
Emanating
a New Life

*The biggest embrace of love you'll ever make
is to embrace yourself completely. Then you'll
realize you've just embraced the whole universe,
and everything and everybody in it.*

—ADYASHANTI

The river of love holds you in its embrace. Your loved ones travel with you as the waters of peace send you gently all the way to the ocean of divine consciousness. There is nothing to do but relax and enjoy. Fill yourself with the grace of the One. Practice taking in its light as deeply as you can.

Celebrate! Enjoy! Anchor this feeling into your cells. Make friends with it, memorize it, normalize it. You are building a new reservoir of goodness and feeding all levels of your being with its life force.

Do not skip this step! Honoring the inner work you've done and then reveling in the sweetness sets up a whole new way of living for you. Expect to take this freshness into the rest of your life, where it will nurture you—just as it's always done, breath after breath, moment by moment… but you didn't realize it. Now you do. You are AWARE and AWAKE. Hallelujah.

People usually consider walking on water or in
thin air a miracle. But I think the real miracle
is not to walk either on water or in thin air, but
to walk on earth. Every day we are engaged in a
miracle which we don't even recognize: a blue sky,
white clouds, green leaves, the black, curious eyes
of a child—our own two eyes. All is a miracle.

—THICH NHAT HANH

Expand Your Blessings

Spend some breaths going deeper and deeper with your circle. Every being who is with you is part of your soul family. Enter the mystical realms together. Imbibe the holy nectar of gratitude and joy.

When you feel ready, begin to expand the purpose of your circle to include a greater vision. In addition to personal healing, add your most cherished spots on Earth for healing: plants, animals, children in poverty, world leaders, specific countries, places hit by earthquakes and tsunamis, war zones … the list goes on.

Since you and I and all beings are the light of the world, we can bless the world. Because our true nature is love, we naturally feel joy and a sense of purpose when we expand our love. Use the power of your circle to move beyond your personal life and its challenges and consciously join the web of life.

The specific areas of the earth that you bless during this part of your forgiveness process will arise without effort. They'll come to you for healing, just as you came to Spirit for healing. You'll notice familiar service projects and personal areas of concern coming up (in addition to some surprises) as you receive the information you need, straight from your intuition.

Floating in the ocean of holiness, you comprehend world suffering as a simple mirror of what has not yet been forgiven by our mass consciousness. In divine love, there is no need to forgive. Yet in the world of humanity, the need rests with us, the awakening tribe. We give our love, expanding it to include everyone and everything. Looking past the devastation but not ignoring it, we see the perfect innocence that pulses eternally, revealing itself as the beauty and wisdom of Mother Earth.

Forgiveness is my function
as the light of the world.
—*A COURSE IN MIRACLES* WORKBOOK, LESSON 62

Closing Your Session with Prayer

At some point, your blessing will feel complete. As always, there is no need to push or work at it. You'll feel fully cooked to perfection and think to yourself, "Good, that's all. I'm finished."

Remaining in delicious contact with your circle and the sweet grace that nourishes you, close your session with a simple prayer of gratitude. Say it out loud, feeling the Presence speaking from within you. Every word is creative, so make it count. This is the closing for your forgiveness session, and you do it as much for your mind as anything else. Say this prayer as a way to let your mind know the session is done. Send your grateful heart out to everyone who participated with you, knowing how much we all need each other in this awakening of love.

Sample Closing Prayer—A Statement of Completion and Gratitude

Beloved One, I give thanks and praise for every-thing I released during this session. I give thanks and praise for all the wisdom and light I received. I give thanks for the teachings that came to me. I will use them well. Blessings and thanks to all of the people who came to my circle today, and deep gratitude for the beings of light who assist me. May all beings be peaceful and happy, and may the healing I received today uplift the world.

Amen (or other closing of your choice).

After the Session— Integrating the Inner Changes

Your healing work continues on all levels, now on the subtle plane of integration. As the days go by, you'll notice opportunities to either support or distort your mission of communion with God consciousness. Which will you choose?

You've moved mountains inside your psyche and been blessed by Spirit for a permanent change. Only YOU can nurture the healing so it goes deep within you. Only YOU can sabotage the goodness with reattachment to past patterns. You *will* be challenged, so it becomes necessary to be very, very conscious and loving with yourself, particularly during this integration stage.

Your energetic signature always sends out messages to the physical universe. Before, the messages were filled with suffering. Now, your messages have done a complete midair flip. Instead of reinforcing your victim story over and over again, you found its opposite and cleaved to its truth.

"I AM holy. I AM loved. I AM love itself. I trust in God. I surrender to God." These are your new thoughts. Miracles unfold from them.

You're floating in the ocean of divine love, ready to receive new friends, new abundance, new creative projects, and a vast amount of heavenly support.

New possibilities and opportunities will enter your life, because you've changed the vibratory frequency of your heart-mind. By letting go of past pain and welcoming the light to enter you, your vibration has shifted, and therefore new adventures are heading your way.

Vigilance will be necessary—not against anything, but to lovingly maintain a clear space for the new YOU to flourish. Keep your space clear by refraining from doing anything that brings you down. You'll know what I mean by the way you feel. If an opportunity or connection feels light, then go toward it. If not, gracefully say, "No, thank you." It's that easy.

To emphasize the point, because it's so vitally important:

DON'T:

- eat a whole tub of ice cream or other foods that don't serve you
- zone out watching TV or surfing the Internet
- get stoned
- get drunk
- indulge in gossip
- schedule a ridiculous amount of work
- spend time with friends who don't support awakening

DO:

- love yourself completely
- eat well
- pray and meditate
- get exercise
- spend quiet time in nature
- find balance at work
- give priority to family and friends who join you in awakening
- listen and follow your intuitive guidance

After a forgiveness session, I feel lighter and more open to new possibilities. I've just let go of a heavy burden, and I want to know how my life will be different and better without it. I'm eager for new adventures. I take care of my body, drink water, get sleep, and keep my thoughts positive. This is my way of honoring my process, and it feels very grounding and expansive at the same time. Forgiveness always opens up access to intuitive guidance. When I follow my intuition, I feel a quickening of excitement travel through my body. I'm trusting, hopeful, and ready for something magical to happen.

You probably know exactly how it feels to go against your intuition. For me, if I eat too much or ingest the wrong thing for my body, or space out watching a stupid TV show, or stay at a party longer than is optimal, I start to feel sluggish and heavy. It's very obvious to me and I know I need to shift gears. I've noticed that my energy can begin to feel drained even during simple conversations if the topic includes complaining or blame, or if I ignore an inner message that I need to leave and be somewhere else.

The most uncomfortable feeling I get is an energetic curdling inside if I say anything unkind about someone else. It's difficult to describe. I look at it as an inner monitoring system. It seems like my soul is getting my personality's attention by pulsing through my blood in a constricted way. I start feeling ungrounded inside. When that happens, I know to stop speaking immediately and find the good in that person instead of the false picture I'd been painting. I focus on the holy essence of the person and the divine union that links us together. That brings my energy back up and feels a whole lot better for my heart. It also keeps me away from gossip and strengthens my friendships.

Living with Your Lessons

If you respect your inner work of transformation, you'll honor it by frequently reviewing the lessons you received during your session. You may want to write them down, paint them, or dance and sing them. Let them grow during times of stillness, meditation, long walks, and dreams.

Whenever it feels right, go back to your forgiveness lists and choose a new person/event to swim with you in the river of love. It's very possible that some people on the lists won't have the charge or tension they had for you before. That's because every person on both lists is linked with you in vast consciousness, aligned with Spirit.

Perhaps you'll find that your lists have shrunk, all because you let the power of love do the healing for you. Or perhaps you'll travel deeper into the blessing of using this process, and you'll realize how many more people belong on your lists! Remember, any memory of fear, guilt, and shame can be healed, using the same step-by-step process. All of your soul themes dance together within the stories you've made of sadness, revenge, and regret. So find the treasures that lie buried beneath the first, most obvious layers. Explore and enjoy your expanding communion with the divine.

The Role of Intuition in Emanating a New Life

As I hope you comprehend to the depths of your soul by now, this forgiveness work was never for you alone. When we wake up, we do it on behalf of all people everywhere, with the intention that the whole world will rise in freedom.

Forgiveness gives us emotional and spiritual reserves. It fills our tank to overflowing. All that goodness can now be consciously used for the benefit of all living beings. The more you let go and let Spirit run your life, the more excited you'll feel to be in service to those around you.

As you unpeel dense layers by using this forgiveness process again and again, you'll stop thinking in a tight, predictable loop of fear thoughts. Instead, intuitive hints will become commonplace—as long as you respect them and follow through with action as they direct!

Make it easy to listen by steering far away from distractions and energy drains (see the list of DON'Ts earlier in this chapter). When your heart and mind are clear, you become a conduit for divine information to reach the earth.

Spirit always gives us messages that are loving, efficient, and good for the whole. But you won't always understand them with your mind, so take some leaps of faith and follow your inner voice. As Margaret Shepard said, "Sometimes your only available transportation is a leap of faith." Following intuitive guidance requires immense trust in the goodness of life. Reach deep within yourself to find this trust. You're building inner muscles and they're getting stronger. Gradually, saying YES to your intuition will become as natural as breathing.

Your intuition's messages may sound like this:

- Take the A train, not the C.
- Go into this store—now.
- Call an old friend—now.
- Get off at this exit.
- That can wait. Sit down and meditate.
- Get out the map. (You suddenly feel like going on a journey!)
- What an amazing dream! I need to write it down.
- What if I move? Go back to school? Change jobs?
- I'm so grateful! Thank you, Holy One.

The more you cleanse your channels, the more your intuition can speak with you. You'll discover new opportunities for service and joy. You'll also find new avenues for your talents and gifts to blossom. Life just gets better, and better, and better, until you have to stretch yourself to make room for how fantastic it can be! This is all done incrementally, as you CHOOSE to make it so. Now that there's more inner wisdom flowing through you, you'll be open to intuitive promptings that come directly from the One.

Your Soul Purpose Revealed

As you become more peaceful, your intuition opens to the point where most (and eventually all) of your thoughts are aligned with Spirit. Cranky illusions are no longer clanging around in your head, taking up valuable space and a lot of your life energy! You get information on a need-to-know basis. There's no need to hold on to impressive factoids and a mud wash of extraneous trivia. Your mind becomes a servant to its Creator, balanced between thinking and resting. You begin to welcome your unique purpose.

A big part of each soul's purpose in coming to Earth is awakening to the perfection of this moment, the Holy Instant, the perfect Now. In addition, we each have a mission that expands our joy. The more grateful we feel, the more we can tap into the specific guidance that brings about our soul purpose. Each person won't become a doctor, a lawyer, a writer, a musician, an electrician, a teacher, *and* an artisan. As humans, we're here on Earth for distinct reasons. Since we can't do it all, we need to choose what we love—and then pursue it to the fullest.

I'm not just talking about your career here. Your soul purpose includes everything you love, including finding aspects of life you didn't even know you love, but when you discover them, your heart catapults with bliss! I'm constantly expanding what I love, and it's a very fun way to live. For instance, I'm musical and I love to dance. I play a bit of piano and flute, but now I find I want to learn how to play the guitar, so I can accompany myself while I sing my songs.

I'm a mother of two amazing, growing children, and mothering is a huge component of my soul purpose. If I did nothing else, my heart would be fulfilled by the joy I receive from caring for and learning from my kids.

But that's not all, because I love to be outdoors as much as possible. I love hiking, gardening, swimming in lakes, snowshoeing, and skiing. I'm not an expert in these areas; I simply love them, and that's good enough. No competitions or prizes needed. No one said I have to be successful in worldly terms (actually, some people said that but I ignored them). I just do it, and love it.

What is your soul purpose in this life? How do you love yourself and the world in the following areas?

- Family
- Career
- Creative arts

- Friendships
- Service
- Education
- Entertainment
- Health and exercise
- Spirituality

I'm not asking this because I'm expecting an answer. The answer is your life, unfolding with creativity as you live it. You are the miracle and the blessing. You are the best YOU there can ever be, and no one else can take your place in the precious web of creation.

The Golden Light

When I was in my mid-thirties, I attended graduate school in Los Angeles. My daughter and I moved there from a small town, and we slowly acclimated to being in a big city. She loved it, but I didn't so much. One of the things that kept me sane during that time was a church some friends turned me on to, called Agape International Spiritual Center.

Agape was packed full of people every Sunday. Run by minister Michael Beckwith, who wasn't famous in those days, the church had a fantastic choir directed by Rickie Byars. One thing I loved about going to church there was the interracial mixture of the congregation. Finally, I found myself in a crowd where black, white, brown, and all people could worship together and send up some great music, too. The devotional joy that permeated the place soothed my soul.

One day, I arrived by myself and sat in the back. I felt happy to rest and pray with a community of people who loved God so much. While I watched the choir, an astonishing thing happened. A woman got up to sing a solo. She was a black woman with a wonderful voice, but what really captured my attention was the way she moved. As I tuned in to her, I realized that she reminded me of an old friend, Sarah, who's also a great singer, but blond-haired and blue-eyed—a very white woman. While I gazed in wonder, the singer and my friend, Sarah, began to merge in my mind. The black woman became my white friend, my white friend became the black singer, and the two women became indistinguishable to me. I know this sounds like maybe I was going a bit crazy, but it didn't feel that way. My inner sight opened up, and it showed me a miracle.

As the song ended and the singer sat down, I looked around the room. Instead of seeing a sea of brightly dressed, swaying and praying different people, all I could see were their similarities. All I could perceive was the golden light, sometimes called the Christ light, in each person in the room. At this point, my mind began to tremble a bit. "I can't find any differences!" I said to myself in awe. "I can't find them!"

I saw clearly how much I'd been seeing separations between people my whole life. It was what I'd been trained to do. Each person came to my world as distinct and different. Each person was subject to my assumptions and projections, just as I was vulnerable to his or hers. But in that moment, I couldn't contact any of that. All that differentiating data swooshed out of my mind (I guess I fell out of my kayak and entered into the river of love again). Instead, as I gazed around the room at hundreds of happy, Spirit-loving people, all I could comprehend was the light within them.

The light shone in each heart as a golden candle of love. Every candle was lit and alive. Every light glowed with the same Source. Each one was IDENTICAL.

As my vision swept the room and I realized that not one person was left out of the golden light, I began to cry soft tears of deep surrender. The grace of the Christ completely enveloped me. My mind hung suspended inside me, unable to think normal thoughts. The beauty and immensity of my vision overtook me. It was undeniably true: every person there was an equal child of God.

At the end of the service, I made my way through the colorful crowd, down to the front where Michael Beckwith was greeting his congregation. When it was my turn to speak to him, I just looked in his eyes and said, "I can't find any differences! I can't find them!" My tears and open face must have told him how expanded I was feeling. He smiled and said with love, "That's a very high place to be." I hugged him and left, overcome with joy in receiving the sacred gift of this experience.

The simple truth I learned that day at Agape, for which I'll always be grateful, stayed with me and served me well. I went on to work as a court mediator with people addicted to methamphetamine whose children had been taken from them, and as a teacher to prisoners in San Quentin who had committed rape and murder. I also worked with a lot of other human beings who didn't have such dramatic stories. Because of that day at church, I knew that every single one of them had an altar in their heart, and inside each altar burned a golden candle of the highest light.

This is the altar we visualize in our forgiveness work. It shines eternally within us and within everyone we meet. We take it out and place it before us when we need help to lay down our burdens. It's wonderful to know that sacred place lives within us all the time. It serves as a special reminder of the healing power of divine love. Let's remember that we are all created equal in this light. Peace will come to our planet as we learn this and share it. Together, always together.

Chapter Thirteen

Reviewing the Process

This final chapter reviews the forgiveness process, so you can see it all in one compact space. It's a shortened outline of the entire book, available to help you to refresh your memory before each new forgiveness session. With it, you'll be fully ready to dive again and again into the river of love.

1. Start with What Is Sacred (Step 1)

Always begin with creating a sacred space. You can do this with prayer. If you don't relate to the idea of prayer, perhaps you can think of it as being sincerely open to a deep spiritual connection. Put yourself into a divine space of trust and reverence. Bring in H.O.W.: honesty, openness, and willingness. Ramp up your faith. Soften your heart. Ask for help from your Creator and blessed beings of light. Be ready to explore.

2. Find and Explore the Knot (Steps 2–5)

Calmly tune in to your body, emotions, and mind. What's bothering you? What doesn't feel peaceful right now? Find out where the constriction lies and examine it with trust. Breathe!

What thoughts connected with the incident/relationship/forgiveness event run through your mind? What does your body tell you? What emotions do you feel? Get to know yourself in your victim story. It's just a story—but you need to slow down to acknowledge it and learn from it. How long has it been accompanying you? Who else is involved? What colors, textures, and images emanate from the knot? What memories rise up for your attention? How are the painful actions of others a mirror for your own behaviors and beliefs (even on a subtle level)?

3. Release (Step 6)

Let your body teach you as each new layer emerges for your attention. Begin to release the old patterns with your breath, learning as much as you can in each moment. Imagine the altar of Love in front of you and lay

your burdens down before it. *Exhale* and allow all your
fear and pain to wash out of you. Open your cell walls,
blood, bones, memories, and all levels of your being.
Let the ocean of spacious Presence take it all. (See
chapter 8 for more details on releasing.)

Feel the flow of tender mercy as it streams continually from the altar. The river of love washes toward you
now, in complete support of your enlightenment. The
altar is the home of the Holy Spirit, the home of your
true essence. You imagine it before you as a helpful
tool for your mind, emotions, and body to be able to
release the old, making room for the One that gives
you life.

This altar lives eternally in your heart, for you were
created with this illumined spaciousness alive and well
within your being.

Give plenty of compassion to yourself as you let go.
Extend the compassion to everyone involved, but only
if you can honestly do so. If this doesn't come easily,
keep releasing guilt, shame, regret, and fear until you
can feel compassion for everyone. (This may take several sessions.)

4. Burdens Disappear and Lessons Replace Them (Steps 6–8)

When you lay down your burdens, you see that they
are illusions (and always have been), made real only by

the constant recycling of painful memories and ideas in your mind. As soon as they reach the sacred space before the altar, they disappear. Divine love does not uphold anything that is not like itself. All illusion must pass into nothingness, because it *is* nothingness.

Reach deep within and find the lessons your soul needs. How has your body changed? What messages does your open heart uncover? What unexpected truths do you discover?

5. The Pause (Step 7)

After you learn your soul lessons, pause and notice how silent you've become. Enjoy the stillness. Nothing is happening. No-thing is happening. It's very peaceful here. Nothing to do, nowhere to go, no one (including yourself) to prove anything to. You begin to merge with the Oneness and you let yourself absorb it. The hard work (though it only seems difficult at first) of releasing is over. Relax.

6. Receive Light and Come Full Circle (Step 9)

By releasing, you made room in your mind, worldview, identity, emotions, and body—now you can take in the newness of increased God consciousness. There's nothing left but receiving. Use your *inhale* breath and drink in the goodness. Let grace travel within you on every level of your being, far beyond what your mind is aware of, trusting the Holy Spirit to heal and fulfill you. When you do this, you notice that the opposite message of your victim story fills you with truth. You receive divine love, deep trust in the perfection of the Holy Instant, and the grace of your true nature.

7. Give Love Away (Step 10)

When you feel like you're overflowing with the blessings you've received, invite loved ones into your circle. You'll know you've fully forgiven when you can welcome the people who challenged you the most with sincere, open arms. They arrive in their spirit bodies, not in their personalities, as equal beings who share a common, sacred essence.

With your circle of soul family, begin giving love away, wherever it is needed or desired. Bless the world, because none of us wakes up alone.

8. Complete with Clarity

End your session with prayers or statements of gratitude and freedom. Breathe, relax, and enjoy. Know that you can use this process whenever and wherever you like. Thank all the beings who supported you, and thank the earth, the home for your embodied soul. Finish by saying "Amen," or "So it is," or whatever conclusion you fancy. This final phrase signals to your mind that the session is over, and a whole new cycle of life has begun.

Surrender

Our entire forgiveness process could be known by another name: *surrender to All That Is*. In Western culture, we don't speak much about spiritual surrender, and tend to think of "surrender" in terms of weakness rather than strength. We know it as a message of loss, especially because we've been conditioned to imagine life as a war zone, with either victory or defeat as the only possible outcomes. The victor wins and receives his or her prize of domination. The loser surrenders his or her power—and that can't be good.

Yet on a spiritual level, surrendering all of our false beliefs to a higher power makes perfect sense. This kind of letting go gives us a conscious choice to realign ourselves with our Creator.

If you believe in your heart that God is good, kind, and merciful—even as God is completely mysterious—then surrender will show itself as a balm to heal all your pain. You will go toward the wisdom that lies beyond your individual mind. With a sense that "giving it all away" is a good thing, you'll practice surrender until your inner muscles know how to do it effortlessly.

Miracles will become commonplace, but never boring!

Notice how when you forgive, you surrender not only your fear, but also the blessings of your life. EVERYTHING—the "good," "bad," and in-between—is offered to the One, where the truth of your being is safeguarded for you.

In the end, all we can do is say, "Thank you, I am blessed," then give this love away.

Simple Instructions for True Happiness

begin by
polishing the diamond

beat back
any continuing insane
insistence upon
entertaining polluted thoughts

clean the air around
the sacred jewel

sweep the floor
light candles and kneel down
pressing your tender forehead
to the ground

then raise your face
to its beauty
look up, and

once you have
completely and entirely
revealed its luminous body
for yourself

climb inside
inhaling radiance
filling and fulfilling
your lungs maximally

relax ... enjoy

then

give
this love
away

Bibliography

Bavolek, Stephen, PhD. *Birth and Beyond* program. Sacramento, CA: February 2012. http://nurturing parenting.com/images/cmsfiles/maleandfemale brainfunctioning2-23-2012-r3.pptx.

Braden, Gregg. *The Divine Matrix: Bridging Time, Space, Miracles, and Belief.* Carlsbad, CA: Hay House, 2007.

————. *Walking Between the Worlds: The Science of Compassion.* Sacred Spaces/Ancient Wisdom, 1997.

Chodron, Thubten. *Working with Anger.* Ithaca, NY: Snow Lion Publications, 2001.

Foundation for Inner Peace. *A Course in Miracles: Text, Workbook, Manual.* Mill Valley, CA: Foundation for Inner Peace, 2007.

Gurian, Michael, and Barbara Annis. *Leadership and the Sexes: Using Gender Science to Create Success in Business.* San Francisco, CA: Jossey-Bass, 2008.

Holub, Ana. *Blessings from A Course in Miracles E-Course.* 2013. http://www.anaholub.com/store/e-courses.

———. *Claiming Your Emotional Well-Being E-Course.* 2012. http://www.anaholub.com/store/e-courses.

———. *Letting Go with Forgiveness E-Course.* 2010. http://www.anaholub.com/store/e-courses.

Levine, Peter A., and Ann Frederick. *Waking the Tiger: Healing Trauma.* Berkeley, CA: North Atlantic Books, 1997.

Lipton, Bruce. *The Biology of Belief: Unleashing the Power of Consciousness, Matter and Miracles.* Santa Rosa, CA: Mountain of Love/Elite Books, 2005.

———. *The Wisdom of Your Cells: How Your Beliefs Control Your Biology.* Boulder, CO: Sounds True, 2006.

Pert, Candace. *Molecules of Emotion: The Science Behind Mind-Body Medicine.* New York: Simon & Schuster, 1997.

Tipping, Colin. *Radical Forgiveness: A Revolutionary Five-Stage Process to Heal Relationships, Let Go of Anger and Blame, and Find Peace in Any Situation.* Boulder, CO: Sounds True, 2010.

Tipping, Colin, and Ana Holub, et al. *Why You Still Need to Forgive Your Parents, and How to Do It with Ease and Grace.* Atlanta, GA: Global 13 Publications, 2010.

Tolle, Eckhart. *The Power of Now: A Guide to Spiritual Enlightenment.* Novato, CA: New World Library and Namaste Publishing, 2004.

Vitale, Joe, and Dr. Ihaleakala Hew Len. *Zero Limits: The Secret Hawaiian System for Wealth, Health, Peace, and More.* Hoboken, NJ: John Wiley and Sons, 2007.

To Write to the Author

If you wish to contact the author or would like more information about this book, please write to the author in care of Llewellyn Worldwide Ltd. and we will forward your request. Both the author and publisher appreciate hearing from you and learning of your enjoyment of this book and how it has helped you. Llewellyn Worldwide Ltd. cannot guarantee that every letter written to the author can be answered, but all will be forwarded. Please write to:

Ana Holub
℅ Llewellyn Worldwide
2143 Wooddale Drive
Woodbury, MN 55125-2989

Please enclose a self-addressed stamped envelope for reply, or $1.00 to cover costs. If outside the U.S.A., enclose an international postal reply coupon.

THE SERENITY SOLUTION

How to Use
Quiet Contemplation
to
Solve Life's Problems

KEITH PARK, PHD

The Serenity Solution
How to Use Quiet Contemplation to Solve Life's Problems
KEITH PARK PHD

Gain a greater awareness of self, learn how to solve life problems, and achieve the life conditions you desire. By demonstrating how to employ calm focus—an alert yet relaxed, optimal state of mind—*The Serenity Solution* helps you approach situations with an increased range of thinking and improves your ability to see all options when facing difficulties.

This clear and effective guide utilizes the strategies that great thinkers, meditators, and problem solvers have worked with over the centuries to achieve mindful results. Discover a variety of easy-to-follow concepts, simple illustrations, and step-by-step exercises to help broaden insight. Do away with your negative outlook, and bring better health and relationships into full view.

978-0-7387-3678-5, 216 pp., 6 x 9   **$14.99**
